PRO·FES·SION·AL·ISM

Professionalism
New Rules for Workplace Career Success

PATRICIA DORCH

Limit of Liability/Disclaimer of Warranty. The author and publisher have used their best knowledge and efforts in preparing this book. This publication contains the opinions, ideas and recommendations of its author and publisher. Neither author nor publisher shall be liable for any loss of profit, or risk, personal, including but not limited to special, incidental, consequential, professional or any other commercial or other damages which is incurred as a consequence, directly or indirectly, of the use and application of any of the contents of this book. The accuracy and completeness of the information provided herein and the opinions of stated herein are not guaranteed or warranted to produce any particular results. The advice and strategies contained herein may not be suitable for every individual, organization or situation.

Dorch, Patricia

Professionalism: New Rules for Workplace Career Success / Patricia Dorch

Copyright © 2012 by Patricia Dorch, **All Rights Reserved.**

No part of this book may be reproduced or utilized in any means, electronic, or mechanical, including photocopying, or recording or by any information storage and retrieval system, without permission in writing from the author.

Bulk Purchases: Minimum Order – **50 Books**
For information about special discounts for bulk purchases please contact Patricia Dorch at:

Website: www.whatisprofessionalism.com
Email: Patricia@whatisprofessionalism.com

Website: www.jobsearch40plusbook.com
Email: Patricia@jobsearch40plusbook.com

Website: www.execudress.com
Email: Patricia@execudress.com

Printed in the United States of America

ISBN-13: 978-0-9816854-4-1
ISBN-10: 0-9816854-4-7

DEDICATION

This book is dedicated to Willie Mae Dorch,
Francine Dorch
and
In Memory of Norman Dorch

ACKNOWLEDGEMENT

I want to extend my personal and sincere thanks to all who have dedicated their time, expertise and advice for this book. Your knowledge and support have contributed to my success.

CONTENTS

Professionalism: New Rules for Workplace Career Success...................1
    Introduction..1
Professionalism: The Smartest Career Decision......................................5
    Professionalism Acronym...5

Chapter One: Professional Interview Etiquette: 17 Rules for Interviewing..7
    Introduction..7
    17 Rules for Interviewing..8
    Interview Professionalism..13
    Ten Tools for Success..13
    Three "Red Flag" Warning Signs for Employers.......................14

Chapter Two: Importance of Professionalism in the Workplace...........15
    Introduction..15
    Seventeen Essential Characteristics of a Professional Employee....16
    Seventeen "Red Flag" Traits of an Unprofessional Employee......17

Chapter Three: Professional Appearance: Show You Mean Business......19
    Introduction..19
    How Do I Look?...21
    Professional Appearance for Men and Women........................22
    Meetings and Conferences..26
    Professional Accessories and Business Tools............................27
    What Not To Wear: Casual Looks for Men and Women..........28

Chapter Four: Fourteen Secrets to Survive Your First 90 Days of Employment...31
    Introduction..31
    Secret 1: Professional Appearance..32
    Secret 2: First Day at Work...33
    Secret 3: New Hire Orientation...33
    Secret 4: New Hire Training..33
    Secret 5: Employment-At-Will Policy.....................................34
    Secret 6: Employment Expectations..34
    Secret 7: Workplace Profanity...35
    Secret 8: Employee Internet Search...35

Secret 9: Company Surveillance..35
Secret 10: Office Politics..36
Secret 11: Political and Social Issues...36
Secret 12: Understand What is Expected of You.....................37
Secret 13: Technology Skills...38
Secret 14: Career Exit Strategy..38
Summary...40

Chapter Five: Act With Integrity In The Workplace............................43
Integrity Characteristics..43
Ten Integrity Principles...44

Chapter Six: Personal Branding: A Career Distinction Tool...............47
Nine Branding Tools for Success..47
Fourteen Principles of Personal Brand Distinction..................48

Chapter Seven: Business Etiquette for the 21st Century........................51
Introduction..51
The Power of Office Etiquette...52
Good Manners for Business Success...55
Cubicle and Open Space Etiquette...56
Cell Phone Etiquette...59
Electronic Mail Etiquette...61
Sharing Too Much Information..64
Personal Hygiene Etiquette..65
Office Party Etiquette...66
Travel Etiquette..68
Bereavement Etiquette..69
        Bereavement Etiquette for Pets....................................72
Disaster and Tragedy Etiquette...73
Summary...74

Chapter Eight: Business Dining Etiquette for the 21st Century............75
Introduction..75
Business Dining Etiquette..76
The Pre-Set Table Setting...76
American vs. European Style...78
When You Have Finished Your Meal...78
Business Table Manners...79

Chapter Nine: Business and Vehicle Expense Accounts: Credit and Gas Cards Etiquette..83
Business Expense Account Do's..83
Business Expense Account Don'ts..84
Company Vehicle, Rental Car or Personal Vehicle..................84

Chapter Ten: Power of Thank-You in Business: 32 Top Reasons to Write a Thank-You Note 87
Introduction 87
32 Top Reasons to Write a Thank-You Note 88
Written Thank-You Notes 91
Summary 91

Chapter Eleven: Interpersonal Communications: Thirteen Strategies for Career Success 93
Introduction 93
Strategy 1: How To Master Exceptional Conversation Skills: Six Secrets for Success 94
Strategy 2: Seven Steps to Improve Communication in Today's Diverse Workplace 96
Strategy 3: Communication and Your Unique Style: Five Tips to Enhance Your Style 99
Strategy 4: How To Create a Great First Impression: Five Secrets For A First Impression 100
Strategy 5: How to Build Relationships: Eleven Strategies to Improve Relations 102
Strategy 6: Real Work Life Stress Management: Six Stress Management Strategies 104
Strategy 7: Communication Strategies for Technical ....107 Professionals: Eleven Ways To Improve Relationships with Non-Technical Professionals 107
Strategy 8: Ten Rules for Active Listening 108
Strategy 9: The Power of Positive Body Language 110
    Nine Secrets for Success 110
    Eight Body Language Tips to Avoid 111
Strategy 10: Workplace Negotiation: Ten Steps To Get What You Want 112
Strategy 11: Better Business Writing: Ten Tips for Successful C ommunication 115
Strategy 12: Powerful Leadership Communication Skills: Twenty One Laws of Leadership 119
Strategy 13: Public Speaking: Why Public Speaking is Essential to Your Career Success 121
    Seven Simple Steps to Speak Easy 121
Summary 122

Chapter Twelve: The Power of Personal Accountability 125
20 Personal Accountability Principles 125

Chapter Thirteen: Intercultural Diversity Skills 129

Chapter Fourteen: Time Management Strategies: Assessing Your Relationship with Time 131

Priorities..131
Goals..132
Planning...132
Personal Time Management Barriers.......................................133
Achieve "Meaningful" Outcomes...133

Chapter Fifteen: Successful Strategies for Difficult Behaviors............135
Introduction..135
Difficult People...136
Strategy 1: Coping with Difficult Behavior............................136
Strategy 2: How to Resolve Conflict.......................................137
Strategy 3: Conflict De-Escalation Strategies.........................138
Strategy 4: Effective Ways to Manage Conflict......................140
Strategy 5: How to Increase Positive Behavior in Others........140
Strategy 6: Three Strategies for Difficult Encounters..............142
Strategy 7: Manage Anxiety in Difficult Situations................142
Strategy 8: Emotional Self-Control..143
Strategy 9: How to Maintain Relationships with Chronically Difficult Behaviors...144
Strategy 10: Rebuilding a Damaged Relationship..................145
Strategy 11: When Your Manager is a Difficult Person..........146
Strategy 12: Seven Strategies to Manage a Difficult Manager.....147
Summary...149

Chapter Sixteen: Teamwork Strategies...151
Ten Teamwork Strategies..151
Ten Ways to Empower Your Team..152
Teamwork People Skills..153

Chapter Seventeen: Problem Solving Strategies....................................155
The PAR Formula (Problem, Action and Results)..................155
Three Steps to Problem Solving...155

Chapter Eighteen: Build Good Relationships: Connecting for Career Success 159
Build Good Relationships with Management........................159
Seven Management Relationship Strategies...........................159
Network at Work..160
Win Inside..160
Why Build Relationships at Work?.......................................160
Benefits...161
Transitional Skills...161
Networking Thoughts...161
Networking As A Way Of Life...161
Develop Your Network: The Smartest Business Decision........162

Chapter Nineteen: Exceptional Customer Service for the Workplace......163
Exceptional Customer Service Strategies...............................163

Chapter Twenty: How to Resign with Grace and Class......................169
    Introduction...169
    Fourteen Resignation Rules...169
    Rule 1: Employer's Resignation Policy...................................169
    Rule 2: When to Give Notice...169
    Rule 3: Letter of Resignation...170
    Rule 4: Meet with Your Manager..170
    Rule 5: Assignments and Projects..170
    Rule 6: Letter of Reference...171
    Rule 7: Competitor Information..171
    Rule 8: Be Prepared...171
    Rule 9: New Employer Privacy Option..................................171
    Rule 10: Get Settled in Your New Job...................................172
    Rule 11: Stay Focused..172
    Rule 12: Professional Relationships..172
    Rule 13: Thank-you Note..172
    Rule 14: Resign with Grace and Class....................................173
    Summary...173

Professionalism: The Smartest Career Decision..................175
    Professionalism Acronym...175

Summary: Professionalism: New Rules for Workplace Career Success..177

About the Author..179

> "*Career success begins with professionalism.*"
> -PATRICIA DORCH

PROFESSIONALISM
New Rules for Workplace Career Success

INTRODUCTION

What is Professionalism?

Professionalism – similar to a brand of a product exists based on a set of perceptions stored in someone's mind. This is an area where perception is reality – what matters at work is what your employer thinks about your professionalism. The good news about professionalism in the workplace is once you master the skills it has tremendous staying power in people's minds. It is determined – career success begins with professionalism – and you have the power to change perceptions.

Professionalism: New Rules for Workplace Career Success is designed to show you how professionalism is associated with the attitude, behavior, and perception of an employee in the workplace. Everything you do regarding your job requires professionalism. You win – your employer wins.

Professionalism is written to provide you with the required tools and coaching your need to be successful in a work and business environment. The purpose of this book is to address the importance of professionalism to be successful. This career resource is for every professional:

- College Students
- New College Graduates
- International Students and Professionals
- Experienced and Inexperienced Professionals
- Returning Workers
- 40 Plus Workers
- Entrepreneurs

Learn how to manage your behavior, appearance, integrity, interpersonal communication, business and dining etiquette and other career survival skills essential to workplace success.

Who Benefits from Professional Employees?

Employers, employees and entrepreneurs in all industries benefit from professional employees. Employers hire professionals to save on hiring, training, reduce turnover costs and increase the bottom line. These cost savings can be substantial and allocated to other areas to achieve the missions, visions and goals of the organization.

What's In It for You?

Professional skills reduce the learning curve for employees to perform work in a timely and effective manner. These skills prepare employees to manage work situations that are vital to career success and increase their income and marketability.

Career success begins with professionalism. The interview is the first test of your professional skills. Hiring managers assess your professionalism based on interview criteria and when making hiring, salary and promotion decisions.

Professionalism: New Rules for Workplace Career Success is an essential career guide for every professional motivated to achieve job growth and success.

"Career success begins with professionalism."
-PATRICIA DORCH

PROFESSIONALISM
The Smartest Career Decision

Professional Appearance – Influence the opinions and perceptions others have of you.

Respect authority, others and our differences.

Oral and written communication skills are essential to career success.

Follow the corporate chain of command – Never go above your manager and complain.

Ethic – Have a good work ethic and take pride in working hard to achieve goals.

Self Awareness – Understand your personal style and adapt to others.

Sensitive – Be sensitive to others perceptions in a multicultural environment.

Integrity – Make the correct choice when faced with a right or wrong decision.

Only use email, texting, voicemail and the internet for company business.

No Gossiping – Do not indulge in office gossip.

Accountability – Take ownership for results whether they are successful or not.

Learn from constructive criticism and feedback.

Interpersonal Communication skills are important to accomplish professional goals.

Success is a result of hard work and persistence.

Manage your time to meet deadlines and accomplish goals.

Copyright © 2012 Patricia Dorch. All Rights Reserved

CHAPTER ONE
Professional Interview Etiquette
17 Rules for Interviewing

INTRODUCTION

Organizations commit a considerable amount of time and resources to interviewing and recruiting employees. They need to identify your *knowledge, skills,* and *abilities* in order to determine whether you are the best candidate for the job.

Demonstrate how your knowledge and experiences can be of value to your employer. Provide examples of how your knowledge, skills, and abilities will help position you as a qualified candidate for the job. Use examples of past performance, experiences, project management, special assignments, internships, hobbies, volunteer work, and other activities to assist you in communicating your achievements.

Your professional appearance at an interview is the first impression you make; your manners and professionalism become important afterwards. Usually, the combination of *appearance, manners,* and *professionalism* help form the interviewer's hiring decision. Learn the rules of interviewing to assist you in being more successful in achieving career goals.

17 RULES FOR INTERVIEWING

Rule 1 – Appearance

Wear a professional business suit with a matching top and bottom in the same fabric. Women have the option of wearing a skirt or pantsuit.

Rule 2 – Be On Time

The interviewer interprets your arrival of fifteen to twenty minutes early, as your interest, commitment, dependability, and professionalism. Being late can show the opposite.

Rule 3 – First Impression

Be kind to the receptionist. Do not smoke, use your cell phone, chew gum, or listen to a portable radio while you are waiting for your interview. You are being observed.

Rule 4 – Outer Coat

Do not wear your outer coat into the interview. Take your coat off after you have spoken to the receptionist.

Rule 5 – Introductions

If the interviewer uses both first and last name during introductions, use the last name when addressing him or her. Introduce yourself by the name you *prefer* to be called.

Rule 6 – Handshake

Give a confident handshake and smile when you shake hands. If you have sweaty palms dry them with a tissue prior to your introduction.

Rule 7 – Sitting Down

Do not sit down until you have been invited to do so. *Ask* where they would like you to sit if there are multiple chairs.

Rule 8 – Preparing for the Interview

- What skills does the position require?
- What skills do you have that relate to the job description?
- What anecdotes can you tell about your knowledge, skills, and abilities that demonstrate your qualifications?
- Before the interview, identify two or three top-selling points you want the interviewer to know about you, and determine how to present them during the interview.

- Bring three copies of your resume, even though you know they already have a copy. Multiple resume copies prepare you for unexpected group interviews.

- Bring a leather writing portfolio and a quality pen with black ink.

- Review your resume prior to the interview. Be prepared to answer questions and explain any gaps during your employment.

- Prepare and memorize five to seven questions you can ask about the position.

- Research the company and department of interest and know who the key people are. Identify who has the power to hire you.

Rule 9 – Vocal Tone

- Match your vocal tone to the interviewer. Do not talk too loud or whisper when you speak.

Rule 10 – Body Language

Avoid signs of negative or power body language:

- Slouching

- Avoiding Eye Contact

- Forced Smiles

- Swinging of Foot or Legs

- Crossing your Legs over your Thigh – may be interpreted as a power statement
- Hand or Finger Movements

Rule 11 – Eye Contact

- Make eye contact, show self-confidence, and answer questions directly with a clear enthusiastic voice. Look directly at the interviewer when answering questions or asking a question.

Rule 12 – Be Positive

- Do not make any negative comments about your current position, status, management, co-workers, or former employers.

Rule 13 – Show You Want the Job

- Show initiative, give examples of your ability to be a team player, work independently, solve problems, and perform the job.

Rule 14 – Close the Interview

- Close the interview by asking the interviewer if they have any concerns about your ability to perform the job. Overcome any objections and *Ask For The Job™* - wait for a response, thank the interviewer and ask about the next step in the interview process.

Rule 15 – Be Natural

- Be calm and natural during the interview closing.

Rule 16 – Thank You Letter

- After the interview email a thank you letter within twenty-four hours and mail the hard copy. Thank each interviewer in a separate letter for taking time to meet with you. Make sure you have the correct spelling of their names and titles. In your thank you letter in bullet format identify two to four points your interviewer liked about your skills. Use *spelling* and *grammar* check, and *re-read* your letter before mailing. Do not use your organizations in-house letterhead or mailing system if you are interviewing within your current organization.

Rule 17 – Follow-up

- Contact your interviewer within one week unless otherwise instructed regarding your interview status.

INTERVIEW PROFESSIONALISM

An interview is the first place job candidates display their professionalism. No matter what level of experience you have employers look for signs to set you apart from your competition. Employers take into consideration the following qualities of new hires.

Ten Tools for Success

1. Professional appearance

2. Positive and enthusiastic attitude

3. Interpersonal communication skills

4. Body language

5. Interview preparation

6. Personal character

7. Ability to answer interview questions

8. Job experience and knowledge

9. Resume appearance – a non-template format

10. References on company letterhead

Candidates who lack professionalism during the interview risk losing a career opportunity to external or internal competition. Listed are warning signs a hiring team may consider when making the employment selection.

THREE "RED FLAG" WARNING SIGNS FOR EMPLOYERS

1. Salary – Candidate inquires about salary prior to receiving a job offer.

2. Promotions – Candidate focuses on promotional opportunities rather than gaining the job offer.

3. Entitlement – Some candidates communicate in their attitude and behavior a sense of entitlement.

CHAPTER TWO

Importance of Professionalism in the Workplace

INTRODUCTION

Professionalism in the workplace is essential to every organization in the 21st Century. Every employer has rules and standards how employees are expected to act regardless of – race, religion, sex, sexual orientation and diverse differences.

Employees should maintain a level of professionalism in the workplace and adhere to employer's written and unwritten rules, expectations and code of ethics guidelines for – adherence to confidentiality agreements, data privacy, conflict resolution, business accountability and other policies and procedures.

The corporate culture has become relaxed over the years with business casual attire this has increased unprofessional behavior and relaxed standards. How you look, act and communicate determines whether you are a professional. Listed are professional characteristics and unprofessional traits you should avoid in your career.

Seventeen Essential Characteristics of a Professional Employee

1. Integrity – make the correct choice when faced with the right or wrong decision.
2. Professional appearance – includes attire and accessories minus visible tattoos and non-religious piercing.
3. Excellent oral and written communication skills.
4. Positive attitude and behavior.
5. Active listening skills – listen to what is said and not said.
6. Good work ethic – completes assignments on time.
7. Self-confidence – has a can do attitude.
8. Self-control – knows how to control emotions.
9. Self-awareness – understand your personal style and adapts to others.
10. Positive interpersonal skills.
11. Shows courtesy to others.
12. Respects others and their time.
13. Business and dining etiquette – good manners and polish.
14. Accountability – accepts responsibility for business decisions.
15. Works independently – flexible and adaptable.
16. Has a sense of direction and purpose.
17. No sense of career entitlement.

SEVENTEEN "RED FLAG" TRAITS OF AN UNPROFESSIONAL EMPLOYEE

Employees serious about their careers should create an action plan to improve their unprofessional traits. To have a successful career and achieve your professional goals address the traits that can prevent you from being considered for employment and promotions.

Seventeen "Red Flags" Traits of an Unprofessional Employee
1. Lacks integrity.
2. Unprofessional attire and visible tattoos and non-religious piercing.
3. Lacks good oral and written communication skills.
4. Poor attitude – negative behavior.
5. Does not listen when others speak.
6. Poor work ethic – does not take work seriously or complete tasks on time.
7. Lacks self-confidence – frequently needs assurance to accomplish goals.
8. Lacks self-control – unable to control emotions.
9. Lacks self-awareness – does not have the communication skills to adapt to others.
10. Lacks positive interaction skills.
11. Does not show courtesy to others.
12. Disrespectful to others.

13. Lacks business and dining etiquette, manners and polish.
14. Lacks accountability – does not make decisions or accepts responsibility for decisions made.
15. Unable to work independently – only comfortable working with others to share responsibility.
16. Lacks a sense of direction and purpose.
17. Communicates a sense of entitlement in attitude and behavior.

CHAPTER THREE
Professional Appearance
Show You Mean Business

INTRODUCTION

Planning your business wardrobe is essential in conveying you are serious about your profession and career. Every professional should have quality business suits and coordinates in his or her wardrobe. A tailored navy blue, black or dark gray suit makes a powerful first impression. Add a business blouse for women and a shirt and tie for men to "show you mean business" in the eyes of management, your peers, customers or clients.

Whether you are working in a boardroom, courtroom, sales field, or in the office, or if you are meeting with clients, attending meetings, or networking, your attention to detail is crucial to your success. Always be consistent in your appearance. A professional appearance is important when representing clients, presenting products and services and building long-term strategic partnerships.

These professions might include:
- Administrative professionals
- Association professionals
- Attorneys and Legal professionals
- Board Members
- Business professionals
- Chambers of commerce professionals
- Communication professionals
- Consultants
- Consulting Firms
- County, State, and Federal Government employees
- Corporate Executives
- CPAs and Accounting professionals
- Customer service professionals
- Education professionals
- Engineering and technology professionals
- Entrepreneurs
- Financial Institutions
- Food Service professionals
- Hospitality professionals
- Human Resources professionals
- Marketing professionals
- Medical and Healthcare services professionals
- Pharmaceutical professionals
- Public Relations professionals

- Sales Professionals – District, General, Regional Management, Executives and Vice Presidents
- Social Services professionals
- Others

HOW DO I LOOK?

Your appearance and everything you say and do should create the perception you are professional, intelligent, reliable, skilled, trustworthy and polished. As you prepare your work wardrobe for each business day ask yourself:

1. Does my appearance make me feel and look respected?
2. Who will I meet with today? Will I be meeting a customer, vendor or visitor at my location or theirs? When meeting with a client at their location on their designated business casual day dress in business attire. You never know what other guests may be attending your meeting without your knowledge.
3. Does my appearance prepare me for unannounced meetings, internal or external visitors?
4. Does my appearance help position me for promotions?
5. Does my appearance attract the wrong type of attention?
6. Does my appearance help identify me to take a leadership role in the absence of management?
7. Does my appearance promote career success or failure?

Listed are *general guidelines* for planning your work wardrobe. Create your own style by adding your favorite colors and accessories that will enhance your appearance and personalize your look.

PROFESSIONAL APPEARANCE FOR MEN AND WOMEN

MEN

Suit or Coordinates (mix and match)
- Solids, stripes, or plaids
- Matching jacket and trousers in the same fabric
- Trousers cuffed
- Non-matching jacket and trousers for a coordinate look

Shirt
- Modified spread collar (recommended)
- Solids, stripes, or plaids
- Long-sleeved for business

Tie
- Solid, stripes or pattern styles
- Business (avoid political, religious, and sexual humor styles)
- Red is the color of power

Shoes
- Lace-ups for business
- Dark color
- Polished and in good condition

Socks
- Dark solid colors or print styles
- Match to trousers or shoes
- Mid-calf or full-calf length
- Cover white socks with dark socks

Belt
- Match to trousers or shoes
- No braces (suspenders) with a belt

Jewelry
- Earrings – not recommended
- Bracelets – not recommended
- Visible necklace – not recommended

Hair
- Cut and styled
- Facial hair trimmed and groomed

Fragrance
- Conservative application
- Be considerate of those who may have allergies

Nail Care
- Manicured
- Neatly trimmed
- Clear polish (optional)

WOMEN

Suits and Coordinates (mix and match)
- Skirt or pant suit in the same fabric and color
- Fashionable classics
- Coordinates

Dresses
- Fashionable classics
- Jacket or sweater looks optional
- Sleeveless (optional)

Blouse
- Solids, small prints or stripes
- Crew neckline, mock or regular turtleneck styles
- Sleeveless (optional)

Shoes
- Leather pump styles
- Closed-toe and closed-toe sling back styles (optional for safety)

- Sandal styles – depends on work environment – (optional)

Jewelry
- No ankle bracelets

Hair
- Professionally styled
- No hair colors that would make you stand out for the wrong reasons.

Hose
- Coordinated with attire
- Bare legs – make a professional business decision (optional)

Makeup
- Conservative application

Fragrance
- Conservative application
- Be considerate of those who may have allergies.

Nail Care
- Manicured or acrylic – no chipped nail polish
- Fashion colors – make a professional business decision (optional)
- No long nails

MEETINGS AND CONFERENCES

Business Casual Attire

In every business situation your supervisor, management, and peers are observing you. Never underestimate the importance of a meeting simply because it has been designated a business casual event. What you wear or the lack of what you wear will affect your career success. Use the event to showcase how well you manage your appearance.

Professional Conduct

During most events time is usually designated for networking or entertainment. When alcoholic beverages are available, although it is a personal and business decision, consider having non-alcoholic beverages. Each person's tolerance for alcohol varies; personalities, language, and behavior patterns can change. From an employer's perspective, if you cannot manage your behavior how can they trust you to manage others in your organization? Any inappropriate actions can be a career-limiting move for your future. Use good judgment, be a good listener and observer, be sociable, and have fun.

PROFESSIONAL ACCESSORIES AND BUSINESS TOOLS

Professional Accessories

Attache or Briefcase Styles (optional)
- Leather
- Dark Color – black or dark brown
- Stylish
- Not oversized
- No Backpacks

Business Tools
- Leather writing tablet – dark color
- Quality ink pen and pencil set (name engraving adds a personal touch)
- Your business card
- Professional name badge
- Cell phone or pager – *Turn off* during business meetings and conferences.

WHAT NOT TO WEAR
CASUAL LOOKS FOR MEN AND WOMEN

There are many definitions and opinions regarding what types of attire fall in the category of business casual. When in doubt, *dress up a notch* rather than on the casual side, or ask your company representative. Listed are *general guidelines* for attire, accessories, and styles that may *not* be considered business casual in your work environment.

Athletic Wear, Athletic Shoes,
Sweatshirts, Tee-Shirts, Sweatpants
Exposed Midriffs, Shorts, Bermuda Shorts,
Tank Tops, Spaghetti Straps, Sun Dresses, Leggings,
Spandex Pants, Exposed Cleavage, Sheer Clothing,
Bandanas, Hats, Ankle Bracelets,
Oversized or Undersized Clothing, Saggy or Baggy Pants
Swimwear, Loungewear, Nightwear Looks,
Military Camouflage Fashion Looks, Moccasins,
Clogs, any color Flip Flops,
Visible Body Art, Tattoos and Piercing

Body art, tattoos and piercing are no longer reserved for bikers and sailors. These forms of non-religious "self-expression" statements have made their way to the boardroom and general population of organizations. However, self-expression statements can cross the business line and form unfavorable perceptions about your professionalism and business judgment.

Body art, tattoos and piercing that have religious, ethnic or cultural meaning fall into a separate category.

If you have questions about your attire, the appropriateness of body art, tattoos and piercing as a "self-expression" or religious, ethnic or cultural statement, contact your company representative or Human Resources Department for clarification.

During business hours, consider covering non-religious "self-expression" statements of body art and tattoos with attire or makeup and remove body piercing that can be visible on your:

- Ankles
- Arms
- Face
- Feet
- Hands
- Legs
- Neckline
- Thighs
- Waistline
- Wrists

Professional appearance is more important in the 21st century than ever before. Appearance and body language always speak first. Appearances influence the opinions and perceptions others have of you. Never underestimate the power your appearance has with those who meet and conduct business with you. In general, people tend to trust, have more confidence, and are loyal to professionals who look good.

Dressing professionally shows you have respect for yourself and for the organization you represent. To a great extent, you are what you wear. *Look authoritative, confident, credible, and successful.* Take the worry out of your professional appearance. Let it be your secret to success.

Show You Mean Business!

If you have questions about your organizations professional appearance guidelines contact your company representative or Human Resources Department for clarification.

CHAPTER FOUR

Fourteen Secrets to Survive Your First 90 Days of Employment

INTRODUCTION

These powerful fourteen secrets have helped many professionals survive their first 90 days of employment and provide a foundation for career growth. These are secrets you are expected to know. No one intentionally plans to fail – people fail because they lack knowledge and information. Knowledge provides the ability for you to apply the information you have learned. These secrets enable you to join the ranks of those who have successfully used these tools and strategies throughout their careers.

Starting a new job is one of the most stressful experiences people face. The first 90 days of employment are crucial to your career success – whether you are a current professional seeking new employment, a college graduate seeking employment for the first time, or a previously unemployed person re-entering the workforce.

Information you provide to an employer about your knowledge, abilities, integrity, and communication skills will be put to the test. Before you speak, think about what you are going to say. Choose your words carefully, and be aware of your body language so that you are not misunderstood. Observe your environment while you are adjusting to your new role, responsibilities, people, and organizational culture.

Manage your internal social network by getting to know multiple people in an organization before you align yourself with any one person or group of people. People judge you by the company you keep. When you are new to an organization, you have no knowledge of other professionals' reputations. In business, what you don't know *can* hurt you. Take your time, be perceptive, and use good judgment.

Maintain a level of professionalism, and marketability in your new and future positions. Be dependable, approachable, and enthusiastic about your new career. Demonstrate your ability to manage and complete assignments and solve problems. Make a commitment to contribute to the success of organizational goals. Listed are the secrets to start a new career.

Secret 1: Professional Appearance

- The professional appearance you presented to get hired should be consistent throughout your career. Always dress for your *next* job.
- Dress professionally every day.
- Attire that is too short, tight, or revealing should not be worn to work.
- Do not dress as if you are going to an

entertainment club, evening on the town, or away for the weekend.

- Uniforms should be clean and pressed. Permanent press clothing usually requires a light pressing.
- If you are unsure if you should wear it or expose it, do not.

Secret 2: First Day at Work

- Arriving fifteen minutes early will make a good impression.
- Be friendly, positive, and focused.
- Prepare yourself for a long day; be prepared to complete new hire paperwork.
- Bring a pen with black ink and a writing tablet.

Secret 3: New Hire Orientation

- Introduce yourself to management and others.
- Be open to changes and new challenges.
- Be aware of your vocal tone when you speak; match your tone to the speaker.
- Bring personal information you need for identification, automatic deposit, insurance and other benefits.

Secret 4: New Hire Training

- Always be on time.
- Conduct yourself as a professional.

- Do not fall asleep in training.
- Participate and volunteer for training activities.
- Do not be loud or have late parties in your room or hotel lounge if you are off-site.
- Be confidential – keep your night out on the town and consumption of beverages to yourself.
- It is not advisable to have personal romances with co-workers or management.

Secret 5: Employment-At-Will Policy

- Employment At-Will policy states either an employee or the company can terminate employment, with or without cause, or with or without advance notice.
- Employment At-Will is usually stated on your job application, and in your letter of offer for employment. If you work for an Employment At-Will employer and require clarification, ask your manager or a human resources representative.

Secret 6: Employment Expectations

- Ask for a copy of your job description if you do not have one.
- Ask questions about your role, responsibilities, and expectations of your performance.
- If you are sick, will be late for work, or have a personal emergency, contact your immediate supervisor and advise them of your situation. *Leave a voice mail message and email message specifying the time you plan to arrive for work.*

Secret 7: Workplace Profanity

There are no excuses or exceptions for using profanity or words that translates to curse words. The use of the word "freakin" or other slang words shows your lack of maturity, character, intelligence, emotional control and professionalism.

Secret 8: Employee Internet Search

- If a new or potential employer did an Internet search on you, what would they find out about you? Do not allow your past or future behavior to sabotage your career.

- Think twice before you participate in social activities that might appear on social networking sites.

- Information on the Internet is difficult to remove. Be prepared to explain comments and pictures that are unfavorable about your character.

- You could risk losing your job or a career opportunity if your employer has concerns about your perception to management, co-workers and clients.

Secret 9: Company Surveillance

More than eighty percent of companies monitor their employees' communication and whereabouts. You have no privacy at work. Be selective with your choice of words in written communication to others. Do not think your personal emails to co-workers, family, and friends are none of your employer's business during business hours.

The use of the company computer for your small business can get you terminated. It does not matter if you are on a break, at lunch, arrive early or stay late on your own time. Keep in mind the computer is the property of your employer.

Employers might observe you using any of the following resources:

- Blog surfing
- Web traffic
- Computer files
- Instant Messaging
- Interior and exterior cameras, visible or invisible to you
- Phone calls
- Emails
- Satellite tracking of a company car, computer or cell phone

Secret 10: Office Politics

- Avoid participating in office politics.
- Stay neutral in your position and comments.
- If someone asks your opinion, simply state you have not made a decision or you have no comment.

Secret 11: Political and Social Issues

- Do not engage in conversations where you are expected to voice your opinion.

- It is advisable to keep your personal viewpoints private.
- Be a good listener.

Secret 12: Understand What is Expected of You

Take time to understand what is expected of you in existing and future career roles. Review your job description with your supervisor, and identify new skills you can learn and others you can improve upon to successfully complete your probationary period. The knowledge and skills you learn will position you for your *next* job.

It is essential you take the *initiative* to meet with your supervisor in 30, 60, and 90 days to gain valuable feedback about your performance. Ask what skills can be improved and what steps are necessary to accomplish the skills they have identified. Let your supervisor be your "champion" for your career development, but never forget that it is ultimately up to you to manage your own career. Listen and be open to critique that will enable you to improve and acquire new skills, use the resources available to achieve department goals, and increase your visibility.

Knowledge, Skills and Abilities (KSAs) / Core Competencies

- What skills will I need for professional development?
- What abilities do I have that require proficiency?
- What additional core competencies will I need to be successful?
- Always make your manager look good.

- Have one-on-one meetings with your manager on a regular basis.
- Contribute to your department goals.
- Identify department priorities and concerns.
- Identify who you can recruit in your "circle of influence" through "networking" to help you achieve your goals.

Secret 13: Technology Skills

- Know what skills are required.
- Be proficient in those skills.
- Learn new skills for promotional opportunities.

Secret 14: Career Exit Strategy

If you determine – before or at the end of your 90-day probationary period – that you are not a good match for the position and no longer want to work for the organization, listed are steps to assist you. These steps also apply if you have accepted a career opportunity with another organization.

Volunteer Resignation – Do:

- Type a dated letter of resignation and present it to your manager.
- Give two weeks notice, and state your last day in the letter.
- Be prepared for the employer to ask you to leave immediately if this is during your probationary period or if you have accepted a job offer with a competitor.

- Ask what you can do to make your transition a smooth one.
- Wish your manager good luck in his or her career.
- Thank your manager for the career opportunity.

Do Not:
- Send your resignation in an email message.
- Walk out without giving notice.
- Brag about where you are going.
- Tell other people why you are leaving.
- Show up late, not show up at all, or call in sick after you have given notice unless you absolutely have to.
- Bad mouth your employer to your next career opportunity.

Termination

If you are terminated during or at the end of your probationary period or at some point in your career, the following guidelines may assist you.

- Ask why you are being terminated if you do not know.
- Accept the termination.
- Do not argue.
- Do not beg for your job back.
- Do not have a bad attitude, use profanity, throw things, or threaten anyone.

- Ask for a "Letter of Reference" on company letterhead if you have been downsized.

Whether you leave on your own terms, are terminated, or your position is eliminated, demonstrate the same professional behavior and attitude you used to get hired. Leave with class on a positive note. You never know when people you have worked with in the past may be in a position to hire, promote or make your life difficult at future career opportunities.

SUMMARY

The most important thing you can do is take "ownership" of your career. Your employer is not responsible for providing all the training, tools, strategics and knowledge you need to be successful. How you present yourself during the first 30-, 60-, and 90-day probationary period will determine if you add value to the organization. Everything you say and do, how you interact, and how you are perceived by others play a role in your success.

If you do not have a college degree, consider obtaining one. Ask if your organization has a college assistance or tuition reimbursement program. If there is no college program, do not let that stop you from obtaining your education. A college degree will positively impact your financial future, worth, and give you the edge when applying and competing for other positions. It's not where you start but where you finish that counts.

Make a commitment to continuous learning. Attend industry association meetings, seminars, training programs, and read books and periodicals. Become knowledgeable about your industry and related fields so you are well rounded.

The time, personal, and financial investment you make in your career is entirely up to you. The only limits you have are those you place on yourself. Establish yourself as a trustworthy, ethical, and credible expert in your field, and your reputation will follow you.

CHAPTER FIVE
Act With Integrity In The Workplace

Integrity is an important characteristic of every professional and your secret to success. A person of integrity is expected to make the right choice when faced with a right or wrong decision. You will be more successful at work and earn the respect of your employer by maintaining integrity. Integrity builds a positive reputation and long-term relationships for you and your employer. Professionals who have integrity possess the following characteristics.

Integrity Characteristics
- Accountable and responsible
- Maturity and wisdom
- Authentic and straightforward
- Behavior is consistent with values
- Character – strength of character
- Values – has clear values when making decisions – knows the difference between right and wrong
- Commitment – delivers on commitments

- Differences – understands and respects differences
- Goodness – believes in the goodness of others
- Respects authority and others
- Self Awareness – understand your personal style and learn how to adapt to others

Integrity is a reflection of a person's character and should never be compromised. Listed are ways you can apply integrity principles at work.

Ten Integrity Principles

1. Employer's Time
- Show up to work on time.
- Do not leave work before your designated time.
- Return from breaks and lunch on time.
- If you are late and do not use a time clock – inform your supervisor of your arrival time and apologize for being late.

2. Do Not Bad Mouth Your Employer
- With other colleagues.
- During and after business hours.
- In public places – such as restaurants, industry organizations, meetings, seminars or workshops.
- On social networking websites.

3. Maintain Confidentiality

- Abide by your company's policies and procedures in your employment agreement.

4. Get Work Done

- Get your work done on time.

5. Company Breaks

- Take only the designated time allowed for breaks and lunch breaks.
- Do not take more breaks than has been authorized by your employer.

6. Mistakes

- If you make a mistake correct it and inform those individuals who needs to be aware of the situation. Making mistakes is a learning process – everyone makes them.

7. You Are Judged by the Company You Keep

- Do not associate with individuals who have a reputation for gossiping or who do not take their work seriously.
- Socializing with the wrong employees will give the perception you act and behave as they do and will limit your career success.

8. Tell the Truth

- Always tell the truth.

9. Be Reliable

- Be reliable and keep all commitments. If you can not keep a commitment notify the proper people in a timely manner. Do not wait until the last minute.

10. Social Networking

- Posting information on social networking sites without company permission regarding your employer, management or colleagues can be a career-limiting move. Refer to your company's employee handbook for clarification.

CHAPTER SIX
Personal Branding
A Career Distinction Tool

Personal branding is a career distinction which identifies and differentiates you from others in your industry with similar knowledge, skills and abilities. You are your brand – your brand advantage is a unique combination of your business qualities, education, professional qualifications and work experience.

Never underestimate the importance of using personal branding for career success. Listed are tools you can use to enhance your brand.

Nine Branding Tools for Success

1. Use a quality ink pen and pencil set. Use black ink for business.
2. Does your company cell phone style and ring tone communicate your business brand?
3. An electronic calendar is recommended. Use a paper calendar as a backup for important dates due to technology failures.

4. Does your computer and cell phone screen saver communicate your brand?
5. Use a writing portfolio in black or dark brown leather with business card holders.
6. Use white tablet paper for business and yellow paper if you are in the legal or financial industry.
7. Always carry your business cards and a quality business card holder.
8. Write your personal branding statement on the back of your business card.
9. Identify a creative and professional way to include your personal brand in emails, reports, and presentations.

FOURTEEN PRINCIPLES OF PERSONAL BRAND DISTINCTION

Think of yourself as a brand. What makes brand YOU unique from brand X?

1. What makes your brand unique from your colleagues?
2. What qualities make you distinctive from your peers?
3. What is your brand strategy to make you "stand out" from others?
4. What are your top three strengths?
5. Stand out by leveraging your strengths and accomplishments.

6. What is your development plan to gain new skills and improve your brand?
7. What is your most worthy personal brand trait?
8. What strategy do you use to problem solve?
9. What strategies do you implement to complete projects on time and within your assigned budget?
10. What positive attributes do others use to describe you?
11. Does your email signature communicate your brand?
12. Do you write your own quotes instead of using quotes written by others?
13. Does your voice mail message communicate your brand?
14. Does your cubicle, workspace, company or personal car communicate your brand?

CHAPTER SEVEN
Business Etiquette for the 21st Century

INTRODUCTION

Business etiquette offers practical advice and tips that are easy to use and helps you come across as a polished professional in a variety of business situations. In today's global multicultural environment being knowledgeable of various forms of business etiquette is essential to workplace success. The ability to demonstrate good manners, get along with others and make others feel comfortable is important to career success.

There are many etiquette questions that might keep you wondering what to do or if you have done the right thing. Being unsure of what to do is uncomfortable. Knowledge builds certainty. You can build confidence by learning how to handle etiquette situations in the office, in open and shared spaces, through electronic communication; at an office party, and traveling on company business.

People gravitate to those who are professional, courteous, considerate, interesting, kind, respectful, and thoughtful.

The etiquette skills you develop will be valuable to you throughout your career and business life.

THE POWER OF OFFICE ETIQUETTE

Office etiquette is a manner of professionalism and personal behavior by employees, to establish positive interaction between management, co-workers, clients and visitors. Knowledge and practice of office etiquette can help you make a positive contribution to the organization by applying the following list of principles.

- Making a telephone call. Organize your thoughts prior to making a call. Begin and end your call with a positive statement.
- Answering the telephone. Always be polite and courteous when answering the phone. Your voice should be pleasant, sincere and express a concern for helping the caller. If the telephone rings when you are working on something important let the call go to voice mail.
- Voice mail. When leaving a message be specific and brief. Do not state your message is urgent if the message is not. Do not leave confidential messages on voice mail. Leave your name and telephone number at the beginning and end of your message.
- Chewing gum. Avoid chewing, blowing, and popping gum during business hours. This behavior is distracting and unprofessional when

communicating with others. Use breath mints or similar products which are good alternative to chewing gum.

- Coughing, yawning, sneezing and belching. Although these are necessary body functions, they can be unhealthy and unattractive. Always cover your mouth or turn away if possible, to protect others from germs.

- Restroom. Always flush the toilet after using it and wash your hands with soap and water before leaving the restroom.

- Makeup. Use your break time or visits to the restroom to attend to your personal appearance.

- Body language. Use positive body language when communicating with others.

- Be tactful with rude people. When others are rude to you, be calm, patient, and courteous. Maintain your composure, and then respond professionally, politely, and positively.

- Personal conversations. Avoid personal conversations with friends, when co-workers and clients are waiting. Personal conversations should be brief and terminated when others approach you.

- Personal office visits. Discourage personal office visits by family and friends, except if there is an emergency.

- Be punctual. All workers should be punctual at the beginning of their workday, returning from breaks, lunch, and attending meetings, conferences, training, and other events.

- Annoying habits. There are distracting habits that others may find unpleasant, such as whistling, picking your nose, tapping your pencil or pen, talking to your computer and others. Identify your annoying habits and avoid doing them at work.
- Respect others. Treat everyone with respect. Never yell, use profanity or disrespect management or co-workers.
- Do not interrupt. Do not interrupt others while they are talking wait your turn to speak.
- Microwave foods. Be careful not to burn foods. Food odors such as popcorn usually carry a scent throughout the office.
- Communal kitchen. Clean up after yourself. Do not expect your co-workers or service staff to clean up after you. Remove your food items from the refrigerator you do not want.
- Company Surveys. Be positive.
- Crying. Attempt to control your emotions in the presence of others. To avoid a reputation of being too sensitive excuse yourself and go to the rest room or another private place.
- Smoking. If you smoke, identify and use the designated smoking areas at work, meetings, conferences, training and other work-related events. Be aware when communicating with others smoking leaves an odor in your clothing and on your breath.
- Holiday Cards and Invitations. Respect your co-workers and management privacy by *not* asking for their home address to mail a holiday card

or personal party invitation. Hand deliver your holiday card or invitation to them at the office to show you are thinking of them at the holiday time. Do not get their address from another source and mail the card to their home address without permission.

GOOD MANNERS FOR BUSINESS SUCCESS

Good manners and courtesies have become increasingly important in the workplace. Manners are a reflection of your professionalism and the company you represent based on your etiquette skills. The use of good manners will increase morale, productivity and leaves a lasting impression in business and client relationships. Use words to promote your manners, professionalism and organization.

- Please
- Thank-You
- Excuse Me
- No Thank-You
- May I help you?
- I'm sorry
- Please forgive me
- Hello
- Good-bye
- It's nice to see you
- I appreciate your help
- Thank you for your help

Manners are appropriate everywhere and improve the professional mood of the office and make it enjoyable for everyone. Listed are some examples of when to use good manners.

Doors
- Hold the door open for someone coming in after you or coming out behind you.

Say thank-you when:
- Someone holds the door open for you.
- Someone allows you to go ahead of them in line.
- If you drop something and other people assist you in picking it up.
- Someone delivers mail or office documents to you at work.

Say hello, smile or nod to:
- Acknowledge the presence of another person passing you in the hallway, elevator, restroom, lunch room, parking lot or other places. Intentionally looking away to avoid eye contact is rude.

CUBICLE AND OPEN SPACE ETIQUETTE

Today's office environment consists of cubicles and open workspaces. Personal office adjustments can mean the difference between a pleasant or frustrating atmosphere. Listed are a few tips to help you be more comfortable with co-workers.

- First Impressions. Your cubicle and open workspace communicates to management, co-workers, and others the type of worker you are. Make sure your space makes a good impression. Keep your area clean, tidy, and maintain well-organized documents. Watch what you post or display, people form opinions of you based on what they see.

- Greetings. Greet everyone who enters your workspace.

- Self-awareness. Use good common sense; do not be too loud, intrusive or unpleasant.

- Cologne and perfume. Many people are allergic to colognes, perfumes and scented deodorants. If you choose to apply fragrance, keep you application light and softly scented.

- Food odors. You may think your food smells good, while others may not. If you eat onions or other foods with strong odors, use mints or brush your teeth and tongue after eating. Be considerate of others and know the rules for eating food or snacking at your desk.

- Confidential matters. In an open environment people do hear and listen to your conversations. Do not talk about confidential matters that you do not want other people to hear. Should you hear confidential matters, pretend that you haven't heard anything, and do not repeat what you have heard.

- Computer screen. Do not look at a person's computer screen without the co-worker's permission and knowledge. Do not use screen savers that make noise.
- Speak quietly. Do not talk loudly over partitions or to co-workers. Go to the person's cubicle or open workspace.
- Speaker phones. Do not use speaker phones at your desk. Other people may be distracted by your voice and your party's voice.
- Personal calls. Use your personal cell phone.
- Phone interruptions. Do not interrupt a person who is on the phone, or use hand signals to distract them. Wait your turn, or come back when the call is finished.
- Interruptions. Do not walk into your co-worker's cubicle or designated open space without permission. When a co-worker is busy, pretend the door is closed. Contact your co-worker by phone or email, or ask if you could meet with them.
- Music. Ask about your organization's policy with regards to music in shared or open spaces. Be considerate of others who might not enjoy your music selection, or who find music distracting at work.
- Prevent distractions. If possible, arrange your desk away from your cubicle opening. Less eye contact can help you eliminate distractions. When you make eye contact with someone at your cubicle, you have opened the door to communication. Be polite, but inform the person if this is not a good time, and arrange for a mutual time to meet.

- Conference room for meetings. If possible, reserve a conference or meeting room when you make appointments with clients or vendors. You want your guest to be comfortable and relaxed; therefore, you must provide excellent service. You should have privacy in order to conduct business without others listening.
- Respect meditation. Do not interrupt someone who appears to be meditating or in deep thought.
- Be cautious with foliage. Remember, others may have allergies to certain plants.
- Respect privacy. When sharing a space, suggest taking lunch and breaks at different times if possible – to allow each of you some private and quiet time.

Cell Phone Etiquette

At work, be mindful of your manager, co-workers, and your ability to get work done without your cell phone interruptions on company time. There are several rules you should consider if you have a personal cell phone at work.

- Cell phones and pagers. Turn your cell phone and pagers off when you are working, attending meetings, conferences, and training and in work related conversations with others. Set your cell phone on vibrate. Check your messages at break time and during lunch.

- Cell phone messages. Acknowledging cell phone messages during meetings is disruptive, rude and unprofessional. Attention given to your messages is an indication to management you are not focused on your job.

- Let your messages go to voice mail. Do not respond to personal texts or voice mail messages during company meetings, seminars, or events. Check your voice mail and text messages during a break.

- It is unprofessional to check or respond to voice mails or text messages in the presence of customers or clients.

- Use your phone for emergency calls. Social calls from family and friends are not appropriate during business hours.

- Identify a private place to make cell phone calls. Do no stay at your desk to talk. Protect your privacy so your conversations are not overheard.

- Never use your cell phone in the restroom. You never know who is in the restroom. People on the other end can hear restroom sounds such as toilets flushing and water running. Respect the privacy of others who may be using the restroom.

- Remove cell phone headsets or earplugs during business hours to show you are focused on your work.

ELECTRONIC MAIL ETIQUETTE

Electronic mail is about communicating with other people. Composing an email message requires that you read it over before sending it. Ask yourself what sort of response you want from the receiver. Time spent making your communication clear is time well spent.

Regardless of the communication used, there are business guidelines and professional courtesies that should be followed. Since electronic communication is not in-person, it lacks voice inflection, tone, body language, and facial expression. Your choice of words is critical to email communication.

Electronic communication has a significant impact on your business skills. You will need:

- A strong vocabulary
- Proper spelling and grammar – re-read your message. Spelling and grammar checks may not always correct words that are spelled or used incorrectly.
- The ability to construct sentences to convey your message.
- Skills to express yourself clearly and concisely, both verbally and in writing.

Subject Lines
- Always include a subject line in your message.
- Avoid creative subject lines. A meaningful subject line provides the recipient with information about your message.

- Stay focused on the subject. The subject is the easiest way to follow the communication. When you change your subject start a new email.

- Uppercase. Do not type your entire email in uppercase. In electronic mail this is considered "shouting" and can be difficult to read.

Replies

- When to reply. Reply to all email messages within twenty-four hours.

- Out of Office reply. Always use your "Out of Office reply" to inform others when you will be out of the office, when you will return, when to expect a reply, and a contact name and phone number of whom they can contact in your absence.

- Replying and changing the subject. When replying to a message put "Reply to" and your subject. If you are replying to a message and changing the subject, start a new message. Changing the conversation without changing the message can be confusing for the receiver.

- DO NOT Reply to all. Do not reply to all when there is no reason for everyone on the distribution list to receive your email.

- CC or Not to CC. There is no such thing as private email. Even when messages are deleted, many software programs can access messages from the hard drive. Before you click on "send", consider the content of your message, and who may eventually read your message without your knowledge. Do not send personal or confidential emails. You would not want your message read or misunderstood by the wrong person.

- Addressing email. Be careful to understand who will be receiving your reply. It could be embarrassing if your personal message ends up on a mailing list for everyone to read.

- No "flame" email. Avoid messages sent in anger. Email is not the place to make negative comments. Negative comments can hurt people and your career.

- No replies. If your message does not require a response, let the recipient know. This can save time for both parties. Say something like "No Reply Necessary" at the end of your message.

- Thanks or OK. Do not send e-mails that say "Thanks" or "OK." One word replies can be interpreted as spam mail. When possible say "thank-you" in person or write a note.

- Website address. When sending a website address, always type it in the form of http:// because some programs will permit the user to click on the Web address to go directly to the site. Without the http:// prefix, some programs will not recognize it as an Internet address.

- Internet lingo. While you may be an Internet pro and familiar with Internet lingo and "emoticons" (like the popular smiley face and others), don't assume the recipient will understand.

- Abbreviations. Do not shorten words by using abbreviations such as OMG (Oh My Gosh), unless you are absolutely sure the recipients understand what they mean. It might be best to spell the words out then put the initials in parentheses so there is no misunderstanding of your communication.

- Attachments. Always use the subject line to inform the recipient of an attached document. Keep attachments to a minimum. The larger the attached document, the longer it takes to download. Consider faxing or mailing long documents, with the recipient's permission. When faxing or mailing documents, take ownership and confirm its receipt with the receiver.

- Forwarded messages. Put your comments at the top of the message. Refrain from sending messages that have been forwarded numerous times, start a new message.

- Signature. A signature usually contains your contact information. Many people use an automatic signature.

- Make sure your signature identifies who you are by listing your full name, title, phone, and fax number.

- Keep your signature short. Four to seven lines is the guideline for maximum lines in a signature.

SHARING TOO MUCH INFORMATION

- Be on your best behavior when you are in the same business and social settings as management.

- When you relax in conversations with management or clients you run the risk of sharing too much personal information about yourself.

- Your manager or supervisor might be in the same age group as you or younger. Always maintain your professionalism and do not drop your guard.
- Protect your privacy.

PERSONAL HYGIENE ETIQUETTE

Body Odor

Consult with your doctor before using any products if you have concerns about your hygiene or health.

Body odor control tips.
- Shower or bathe at least once per day.
- Use antiperspirant deodorant and body powder.
- Astringents used under the arms kill bacteria.
- Shaving or trimming underarm hair helps eliminates a breeding ground for bacteria.
- Launder clothing more often. Wash clothes using an odor-fighting detergent. Dry clean clothes on a regular basis.
- If the odor is stained in your clothing it will be difficult to remove the smell, even if you wash or use dry cleaning.
- Spicy foods, caffeine, and stressful situations will intensify body odor.
- Freshen-up. During the day freshen-up those areas of your body, which require more attention.

Halitosis (bad breath)

Consult with your dentist if you have questions about the appropriate care for yourself. Bad breath can be caused by:

- Diet
- Gum disease
- Improper hygiene
- Smoking
- Some medications

Control bad breath by:

- Scheduling regular dental check-ups for consultation
- Using breath mints
- Using mouthwash
- Drinking plenty of water
- Using a tongue scraper

OFFICE PARTY ETIQUETTE

During the year you may be invited to your company office party. No matter how festive the occasion, it's important to remember this is business. Office parties and functions are the most likely career killers. Sometimes current and potential employees behave inappropriately. Do not risk your career success by damaging your professional reputation at any occasion.

The following advice will ensure a smooth and enjoyable celebration:

- Attend the office party. Attending the office party is the *politically correct* thing to do, and shows you are a team player. No matter how formal or informal the occasion, there is someone *always* watching your behavior and noting whether or not you attend.

- Who should attend? Clarify who is invited with the party coordinator. Spouses, children, boyfriends, and girlfriends are not always invited.

- Arrival and departure. Arrive on time and avoid arriving twenty minutes before the party ends just to make an appearance. Do not be last to leave. Say goodbye to company officials. Your error in judgment will be noticed.

- Eat and drink. Eat something light before the party. If alcohol is served, drink in moderation and responsibly. *It may be best not to drink at all.*

- Dress appropriately. Dress professionally for the occasion. Anything *short, tight,* and *revealing* should stay at home.

- Introduce yourself. Your company party may be the only time you see the CEO, VPs, and other company officials in person. This may be a good opportunity to become visible.

- Conversations. Keep conversations light and happy. Do not use this occasion to criticize others or discuss work-related problems.

- Business romances. Work and work-related activities should involve no public display of affection. If you meet someone of interest,

discreetly exchange your name and phone numbers and connect at a later date.
- Dancing. Remember, you are at work; be conscious of inappropriate body movements.
- Network. Use the occasion to strengthen new and old business acquaintances.

TRAVEL ETIQUETTE

Many employees will attend training, conferences, meetings, or special events at other locations. Unless your are management, you might be assigned a roommate. Listed are tips to show your professionalism and have a positive roommate experience.

Tips for Roommates
- Communicate. Both talking and listening will be the key to a good roommate relationship.
- Identify space. Identify who will have the left and right side of the bathroom, shared sleeping area, and closet. This will allow each person to have his or her own space.
- Clean up. Make sure your leave the bathroom; shower, sink, and toilet clean for the next person.
- Neatness. Pick up your clothes, accessories, and towels, and put them in a designated area.
- Borrowing. If you have to borrow something, always ask permission first. Return it in the same condition in which it was borrowed. If you

damage or lose something you borrow, you are responsible for replacement.

- Lights out. Be considerate of others who may go to bed or awaken earlier than you do.
- Quiet time. Discuss with your roommate if you want to increase the volume of music, entertain other guests, or have a party.

BEREAVEMENT ETIQUETTE

During your career, you might experience the loss of a co-worker, manager, company executive, a personal family member, or friend. We often do not know what to do when someone has experienced a loss. It is important to remember doing or saying something is better than doing nothing at all.

The following are bereavement etiquette strategies for sending condolences:

Phone Calls

Phone calls may be intrusive unless you are close to the co-worker or family. The bereaved do not want the burden of making repeated polite conversation with people on the phone during their loss and healing process.

If you decide to make a phone call, make it short. Ask if you or your organization can do anything to assist the family.

Written Notes

You may decide to send a personal written note or sympathy card to the co-worker who has experienced a loss.

Email

Email is acceptable to send to a co-worker or manager who has lost a family member or close friend. Although the co-worker or manager may not receive it until they return to work, it shows you were thinking about them during their loss.

Donations

Send a donation to an organization in the deceased name is an option to sending flowers.

- Find out the charities, foundations, or associations to which the family would like you to make a contribution on behalf of the deceased.
- The charity, foundation, and association websites will guide you through the donation procedure, or you can contact them directly for donation information.

How Much Do you Donate?

- The amount you donate depends on your relationship with the person or organization.
- Send a note to the family on company letterhead and explain a donation has been made. Listing the amount of the donation is optional.

Cultural Sensitivity

Different bereavement customs are practiced by different cultures. To determine the appropriate practice:
- Find a website with information.
- Ask for help from those of the same culture.

Follow-up

Depending on cultural practices, follow-up in a few weeks to let the bereaved know you are thinking of them.

If you send flowers, a note or poem may be used upon your good judgment.

Healing After a Loss

For you (the bereaved)
- Ask for help if you need it.
- Express your feelings to others.
- Be aware of your physical needs.
- Learn more about grief.
- Give yourself time to heal.

For co-workers, family, friends, and others who care
- Be a good listener.
- Be available for the bereaved.
- Be patient.
- Let the person cry.

- Provide support.
- Do not say you know how they feel.

Ask How You Can Help

- Helping or taking over a task at work might be helpful and appreciated.
- Be specific in your offer to help, and follow up with action.

Danger Signs

Observing the following signs may mean the bereaved person needs professional help.

- Depression
- Lack of personal hygiene
- Physical problems
- Sleeping disorders
- Substance abuse
- Substantial weight loss
- Talking about suicide

Bereavement Etiquette for Pets

Pets for many people are considered family members. The death of a pet can affect your life more that the death of a relative or friend. *It is not recommended you announce the reason for not attending work; meeting with a customer or client is due to the loss of your pet. In business perception is everything.* Listed are tips to help you, a co-worker, family, or friend through the loss of their pet:

- Sympathy Card. Send a pet sympathy card to a co-worker, family member, or friend who has suffered a pet loss.
- Email. Send an email expressing sympathy for the loss of a persons pet.
- Pet cemetery. Contact your local pet cemetery for services they may provide.
- Write a poem. Writing poetry about your pet may be relaxing.
- Scrapbook. Preparing a scrapbook of favorite photos is comforting.
- Distractions. Spending time with family and friends will help distract you from your loss.

DISASTER AND TRAGEDY ETIQUETTE

Disasters and tragedies come in all forms and can disrupt the work and life of co-workers, family, and friends. Both are unpredictable, and therefore no one can plan for their prevention.

At work, co-workers are often faced with feelings of "what should I do?" when informed a tragedy has touched the life of a fellow employee. Helping others in their time of need is the first step. You don't have to be a friend or know someone personally to offer assistance. Listed are easy tips to help people who have experienced unfortunate situations.

- Give comfort and support.
- Be a good listener. Listening to those who are suffering is a good prescription for healing.
- Be hands-on. Ask how you can make a difference. Depending on the situation, you might be asked to take over a work assignment, collect donations, prepare flyers, help locate temporary shelter, contact local and out-of-state family members, and others.

Respect People Who Experience a Disaster or Tragedy

- Understand that people need time to grieve their experience.
- Be available if they need a shoulder to lean on.
- Do what you can to help ease their pain.
- Ask others to help if you need assistance.

SUMMARY

Professional etiquette helps to create the confidence you need in order to improve your behavior in the workplace, by knowing how to deal with situations both ordinary and exceptional, and by being able to appreciate good etiquette in others.

Etiquette is a key factor in dealing with all customers, whether internal or external and will most certainly have a determining factor in the progress of your career.

CHAPTER EIGHT

Business Dining Etiquette for the 21st Century

INTRODUCTION

Everyday a business meal is used for breakfast, lunch, teatime, and dinner. Professionals use business meals for interviews, performance reviews, promotions, meetings, conferences, meeting clients, presenting products and services, networking and other reasons.

Table manners play an important role in making a positive impression in business. Visible signs of your manners are essential to your professional success. Your social skills are on display; never assume others will not notice or be understanding of poor table manners. Polished table manners speak volumes about your professionalism, and can take your career or business to another level.

BUSINESS DINING ETIQUETTE

Napkin Use
- Place your unfolded napkin on your lap.
- The napkin remains on your lap during the entire meal.
- Use your napkin to gently blot your mouth during your meal.
- At the end of the meal, place your napkin on the right of your dinner plate.
- Do not refold or bundle up your napkin.

Ordering
- Ask your server questions you might have about the menu.
- As a guest, do not order one of the most expensive items on the menu.
- Women's orders are usually taken before men's.
- Your server will determine how to take your order.

THE PRE-SET TABLE SETTING

As a general rule, liquids are on your right side and solids are on your left.

To The Right

- Glassware
- Cup and saucer
- Knives and spoons
- Seafood fork, if seafood is included in the meal

To The Left

- Bread and butter plate
- Small butter knife is placed horizontally across the top of the plate
- Salad plate
- Napkin and forks

Use of Silverware

- The rule of silverware usage is work your silverware from the outside in.
- Use one utensil for each course.
- The salad fork is on the outer left, followed by your dinner fork.
- Your soup soon is on your outer right, followed by your dinner knife.
- Dessert spoon and fork are placed above your plate or brought out with the dessert.

American vs. European Style

American Style
- Cut food by holding your knife in the right hand and the fork in the left hand.
- Change your fork from your left hand to your right hand to eat, with the fork tines facing down.
- If you are left-handed, keep your fork in your left hand, tines facing up.

European (or Continental) Style
- Cut food by holding your knife in your right hand while securing your food with your fork in your left hand.
- Your fork remains in your left hand, tines facing down.
- Your knife is in your right hand.
- Eat small pieces of food.
- Pick food up with your fork, which is in your left hand.

When You Have Finished Your Meal
- Do not push your plate away from you.
- Lay your fork and knife diagonally across your plate.
- Place your knife and fork side by side with the sharp side of the blade facing inward. The fork tines should face down. The knife and fork should be positioned at 10 and 4 o'clock.

- Do not place used silverware back on the table. Place it on the saucer. Unused silverware should be left on the table.
- Leave a soup spoon on your soup plate.

BUSINESS TABLE MANNERS

- Doggy bag: Do not ask for a doggy bag if you are a guest. Reserve doggy bags for informal dining.
- Finger foods: Finger foods can be messy and are best left for informal dining. Order foods that can be eaten with a knife and fork.
- Alcoholic beverages: Use good judgment. Behavior patterns tend to change when you drink. If you are employed, drinking during business hours is not recommended. Use good judgment.
- Smoking: Do not smoke while dining out; this might offend your guest. People form opinions of you based on what they see and smell.
- Body language: Do not slouch; sit up straight at the table.
- Resting your hands: When you are not eating, keep your hands in your lap or resting on the table, with your wrists on the edge of the table. Elbows on the table are acceptable between courses but not during meals.
- Food Seasoning: Do not season your food before you have tasted it.
- Chewing: Never chew with your mouth open or

make noises when you eat. Do not talk with your mouth full.

- Slurping your soup: Do not slurp your soup from the spoon or pick the bowl up to your mouth. Spoon your soup away from you when you take it out of the bowl. Do not blow your soup if it is hot; wait for it to cool.

- Food between your teeth: If you cannot remove the food between your teeth with your tongue, excuse yourself from the table and go to the rest room where you can remove the food in private. Those foods might include broccoli, spinach, fresh ground pepper, or corn on the cob.

- Eating bread and rolls: Tear and butter one piece at a time.

- Conversation: Engage in lively conversation free of controversial topics such as politics, race, religion, or sex.

- Leaving the table: If you leave the table during the meal, simply excuse yourself.

- Out of your reach: If you need something on the table that is out of your reach, politely ask the person closest to the item to pass it to you.

- Fallen silverware: If a piece of silverware falls on the floor pick it up if you can reach it. Politely ask the server to bring you a replacement.

- Food and liquid spills: If food spills off your plate, pick it up with a piece of your silverware and place it on the edge of your plate. If a liquid spills, clean it up as much as you can, and limit the attention you draw to yourself.

- Bad food: Never spit out a piece of bad food or gristle into your napkin. Discreetly remove the food from your mouth with your utensil and place it on the edge of your plate. You may choose to cover it up with other food on your plate.
- Dry mouth: Keep your mouth moist. A dry mouth can cause white saliva deposits to appear on your lips, and in the corners of your mouth without your knowledge.

CHAPTER NINE

Business and Vehicle Expense Accounts, Credit and Gas Cards Etiquette

Some organizations issue a company vehicle, credit cards or require you use your personal vehicle, rental car and credit cards for business reimbursements. The company vehicle or rental car should be used for authorized use only. Use credit card etiquette at conferences, events, training, entertaining customers, and conducting regular business when expenses are authorized. Listed are general guidelines to help you manage your business expenses and adhere to company policies and procedures.

Business Expense Account Do's:

- Turn expense reports in by the due date.
- Use a mileage log to document authorized business mileage to and from your work destinations.
- Document meals and entertainment with customers and clients. Include complete names and titles of individuals who attend on your expense receipts and report.

- Organize expenses by date.
- Neatly attach all documentation and receipts before you turn them in.
- Completely fill out your expense reports. Incomplete reports may delay reimbursements and approval.

Business Expense Account Don'ts:
- Do not order the most expensive food on the menu for meals. You may consider ordering non-alcoholic beverages when using a company expense account. Use good judgment based on the business situation.
- Do not abuse credit cards purchases by expensing the most expensive purchases.
- Do not expense personal meals, entertainment or gas for family or friends.
- Do not let unauthorized individuals use company credit cards.
- Do not use company gas card purchases for family or friends vehicles.

Company Vehicle, Rental Car or Personal Vehicle
- Do not let unauthorized individuals drive your company vehicle or rental car.
- Keep your company car, rental car or personal car clean during business hours.
- Maintain regular scheduled vehicle maintenance on personal time.

- Report all accidents to your supervisor or manager and follow company policies and procedures.
- During business hours remove anything not related to business.
- Do not go to places with a company vehicle where it might create an embarrassing situation for you and your employer if a picture of you or the vehicle was on the internet.
- Do not leave important or confidential company valuables in the car if you use valet parking.
- Do not share with friends or extended family members unauthorized company products or services.

Expense account and vehicle abuse are one of the top reasons employees are terminated. Perceptions are not easily changed. If your expenses and spending behavior are questionable – they may be "red flagged" for regular review by management.

If you have questions about the appropriateness of an expense ask your manager prior to expensing the item.

When in doubt if you can expense an item – do not or you may choose to pay for it as a non-business expense.

> *"Anyone who forgets to write a thank-you note does not value the power of gratitude."*
>
> \- PATRICIA DORCH

CHAPTER TEN

Power of Thank-You in Business 32 Top Reasons to Write a Thank-You Note

INTRODUCTION

Did you say thank-you?

A "thank-you" note is a powerful business tool and gesture of professional courtesy. The regular practice of writing a thank-you note will help you be remembered and enhances your personal brand and chances for success.

Write a "thank-you" note to interviewers, managers, co-workers and others. An email thank you lacks formality – however it can be used when time is an issue or email is the best method of communicating. Once you have stated "thank you" in your note or email do not say "thanks again" in your closing.

Often people do not know what situations they should consider writing a thank you note. Showing gratitude and appreciation by using two simple words "thank-you" has the power to transform your career. Listed are some useful guidelines to write a thank-you note and promote your success.

It's the little things that count, and pay off in a big way.

32 Top Reasons to Write a Thank-You Note

1. *Administrative Professionals Day* – Show your appreciation to the administrative staff that provides support to help you achieve organizational goals.

2. *Advice* – Someone provides advice that is instrumental to your success.

3. *Bonus or Salary Increase* – To acknowledge a bonus or salary increase.

4. *Book Author* – Express your thanks for an autographed book at a book signing event or if you receive a book with a marketing proposal. Write a thank-you note or send an email thank you to a friend who is an author to show your appreciation and etiquette for the gift.

5. *Business Agent.* A business agent is successful in gaining contacts, contracts or a platform of exposure that will benefit you professionally or financially.

6. *Clients* – Clients provide new and repeat business, referrals, and references for additional business.

7. *Coach* – A person who provides business, career, inspirational, life or sports services.

8. *Committees and Boards* – You have been invited to participate on a committee or board that may have immediate or long-term benefits for your career.

9. *Co-Workers* – Co-worker provides assistance that was important and necessary but not expected, requested or required.

10. *Customers* – Show appreciation for business and customer loyalty.

11. *Employees* – Show appreciation for a job well done.

12. *Expert Host* – You have been invited to speak on a topic which you are an expert.

13. *Gifts* – Be gracious when receiving gifts, even if you do not like what you receive.

14. *Information* – Someone provides valuable information that saved you time and or money to gain the information.

15. *Interviewer* – Write a thank-note to your interviewer for the opportunity to interview for a position which you applied and when you have accepted the job offer.

16. *Job Search* – Someone who was influential in your job search.

17. *Managers and Supervisors* – Managers and supervisors provide support, feedback, promotional opportunities and leadership for your career.

18. *Mentor* – Mentors who provide advice that is instrumental to your career success.

19. *New Hire Team* – All people on a new hire committee that selected you for employment.

20. *Office Etiquette* – People who may have provided support during bereavement, a personal tragedy or assistance with a project. You may consider writing an individual or group thank you note.

21. *Party or Event* – People who hosted a party or event for you.

22. *Personal Delivery* - A person hand delivers an important package or document to someone on your behalf.

23. *Personal Friends* – Friends who support you or do something special for you.

24. *Prayer* – A person or group provides prayer to comfort you during your time of need.

25. *Radio or Television Host* – You have been invited to be a guest expert on a radio or television show.

26. *Recommendation* – A person who recommends you for something of value.

27. *Reference* – A person provides a reference for employment or something you will gain as result of their reference.

28. *Referral* – Someone provides a career, personal or business referral whether or not there was a positive outcome.

29. *Resignation* – Write a thank you note to your manager and co-workers for their support during your employment.

30. *Social Network.* You are introduced to key people that can position you for a personal or professional success.

31. *Speaker Host* – You have been asked to be a guest speaker at an event that can advance your career.

32. *Vendors and Contractors* – It is often teamwork that helps you achieve your departmental goals.

Written Thank-You Notes

- Written thank-you notes are more personal and convey special appreciation.
- Short two or three line messages are sufficient.
- Timely thank-you notes are sincere and easier to write when done within one week.
- Make a specific reference to the gift or contribution your organization or business received.
- Thank-you customs: Thank you gifts and customs vary based on culture.
- Thank-you notes are for "thank-yous," not for business discussions.

SUMMARY

There are many people with whom you interact daily. Saying "thank-you" is important and effective in building relationships in interviews, business, with co-workers, internal and external customers, and clients. Thanking others makes a positive reflection on your business or organization's ability to succeed and achieve goals.

Writing a thank-you note is the easiest and most powerful strategy you can use to achieve success. A thank-you card can be displayed on a desk as a reminder of your appreciation and admired by others.

At work and in business a personal thank-you note shows your business etiquette, personal brand, appreciation and professionalism. Never underestimate the power of a thank-you note in business – it never goes without being noticed.

CHAPTER ELEVEN
Interpersonal Communication
Thirteen Strategies for Career Success

INTRODUCTION

Clear communication is an essential element of business success in the 21st Century. You can improve the quality and style of your interpersonal relationships by making a commitment to improve your skills. Interpersonal skills allow you to improve your listening skills, leadership skills, build relationships, and understand cross-culture communication and other related communication strategies for success.

Learn how to develop good conversations, manage your body language, mind and words to improve your communication. Use powerful communication strategies that will improve your self-esteem, personal confidence and professional relationships.

STRATEGY 1

How to Master Exceptional Conversation Skills
Six Secrets for Success

Good conversation skills are important in every aspect of your career. The ability to be comfortable and hold conversations with people of different cultural backgrounds and multiple business levels will position you for advancement.

Never allow a persons position or title keep you from holding a business or cordial conversation. Every conversation consists of three key elements to be successful. First, be a good listener, second, do not interrupt the speaker, three, wait until the speaker asks for feedback or gives you a cue to participate.

Start with a topic you have in common – work or business – then direct the topic in the direction you want to go. Conversations about the weather, current events, holiday events or a hobby are general topics. At work be careful not to be critical of company policies and procedures or co-workers during your conversation. Learn the secrets that will improve your conversations with professionals.

SIX SECRETS FOR SUCCESS

Secret 1: Active Listening
- Listen to understand the speaker.
- Listen for what is not said – read between the lines.
- Do not interrupt.
- Listen for cues to participate in the conversation.

Secret 2: Focus

- Focus on the speaker.
- Observe the speaker verbal communication and non-verbal body language.

Secret 3: Show Emotion

- Nodding your head.
- Lean forward to show interest.
- Timely interjections.

Secret 4: Give and Take Conversations

- Do not control the entire conversation.
- Do not speak longer than 3 minutes.
- Allow others to participate in your conversation.
- Do not interrupt an existing conversation.
- Do not change the conversation of the group you have just joined.

Secret 5: Criticism

- Do not criticize others in public or private.
- Offer your opinion without criticizing their point of view.
- Ask probing questions that might help you better understand their perspective.

Secret 6: Sex, Religion and Politics

- Do not discuss or participate in topics of sex, religion or politics.
- Keep personal views to yourself – your opinions can make or break your career.
- When in the company of those who are discussing these topics practice good listening skills.
- When asked for your opinion – state "I have no opinion at this time." This would be a good time to excuse yourself and move on to another conversation.

STRATEGY 2

Seven Steps to Improve Communication in Today's Diverse Workplace

The workforce is a combination of employees who come from domestic and international backgrounds. The challenge is to ensure communication is understood regardless of our unique cultural differences. Diversity encourages us to learn and understand different types of spoken English in verbal and non-verbal communication. Here are simple steps to improve diverse communication at work.

SEVEN SIMPLE STEPS TO COMMUNICATE

Step 1: Communicate your Message

- Analyze your audience and determine the best method to communicate your message.

- Consider using different cultures to join you in communicating your message to avoid misunderstandings.

- Using different cultures to communicate will provide an atmosphere for questions and answers.

Step 2: Praise Communication

- Identify the preferred way to praise employees based on cultural differences.

- Some cultures prefer praise in public while others prefer it privately.

- Some cultures prefer they are not praised for performance.

Step 3: Reprimand Communication

- Reprimand employees privately to avoid personal embarrassment.

- Explain to the employee what specifically they did wrong and confirm they understand to avoid future mistakes.

- Counsel employees about what the expectations are and strategies they can use to improve future situations.

Step 4: Train International Employees

- It is essential to communicate company policy, procedures, rules and guidelines to employees during the hiring process.

- Confirm employees understand the importance of adhering to company polices.
- Invest time in providing ongoing training to prevent confusion and misunderstanding.

Step 5: Assign Mentors

- Assign mentors to help employees adjust to their work environment.
- Identify social mentors to help the employee and their families adjust to their new culture.

Step 6: Open Door Communication

- Explain the benefits of open door communication.
- Encourage employees to communicate their concerns and provide feedback.
- Select representatives who can speak on behalf of cultures that are not accustomed to open door communication.

Step 7: Jargon

- Some employees may have difficulty understanding jargon such as requesting a "John Hancock" (their signature) on an offer letter of employment.
- Use language that can be understood by all cultures to prevent a communication gap.

STRATEGY 3

Communication and Your Unique Style
Five Tips to Enhance Your Style

Identify someone you admire who has excellent communication skills. What do you like about the way they communicate to you and others? Over a period of time slowly incorporate what you like about their style with yours and make it uniquely you. Listed are useful tips to personalize your style.

FIVE TIPS TO ENHANCE YOUR STYLE:

Tip 1: Listen

Listen to your speech, choice of words, and tone of your voice and be aware how you are communicating through your body language.

Tip 2: Change Behaviors

Change personal behaviors that are out dated or are no longer effective.

Tip 3: Build Rapport

Slightly match your movements and responses to the speaker, however do not do everything he or she does. For example you might start by slowing your speech, or giving short answers to questions. These small but important changes can help you build rapport and improve your communication.

Tips 4: Alternate your Style

Learn how to personalize your communication style by alternating your style for individual and group settings. Be careful not to share to much personal information in any business setting.

Tip 5: Do Not Criticize Others

Do not criticize others who communicate differently. Listen, be patient, sincere and embrace unique differences.

STRATEGY 4

How to Create a Great First Impression
Five Secrets for a First Impression

It takes only a few seconds for someone to form an impression of you based on your *appearance, body language, communication skills, demeanor* and *mannerisms*. At every encounter you make a first impression and set the tone and expectations for future relationships. Listed are secrets that will make your first impression successful.

FIVE SECRETS FOR A FIRST IMPRESSION:

Secret 1 – Physical Appearance

The key to a good first impression is to present yourself appropriately. Create a powerful impression to set the stage for what can be expected from you in the future.

Wear attire that is appropriate for the situation whether it be for a business, business casual, casual or formal occasions.

Secret 2 – Be On Time

To make a good first impression plan to arrive 15-20 minutes early for an interview, meet your contact, attend a meeting and allow one hour if you are a presenter. There is no such thing as a "good excuse" anymore for being late. Arriving early will save you embarrassment and is the right move in making a positive first impression. Being on time gives you time to relax, socialize with others and focus on the purpose of your meeting.

Secret 3 – Be Yourself

Relax so others in your company will be an ease. Be calm, confident and in control. Your interpersonal skills will set the foundation for your relationship with others.

Secret 4 – Be Confident

Positive body language will communicate you are confident and have self-assurance. Make direct eye contact and greet others with a firm handshake.

Secret 5 – Smile

There is nothing like a smile to make a good first impression. A sincere smile will put you and others at ease.

STRATEGY 5

How to Build Relationships
Eleven Strategies to Improve Relations

At work building good effective relationships is important to career success. Build relationships that are positive, cooperative and respectful. All parties should work together to accomplish the goals of the organization. To manage your relationships use strategies that will improve business relationships.

Eleven Strategies to Improve Relations

1. Trust

- Trust is the first step in building relationships.
- Trust is earned.
- Until a person is considered to be trustworthy you can not strengthen a relationship.

2. Listening

- Listen to understand others feelings and position.
- Listening is the underlying skill to build good relationships.
- Listen and observe without premature judgment.
- Listen for mutual understanding.
- Listen for what is not said.

3. **Respect**
    - Respect is a critical component of good relationships.
    - Respect is the foundation of strong relationships for yourself and others.
    - Treat everyone with respect.

4. **Invest Time**
    - Invest time and energy to understand the other person's needs.
    - Make an attempt to manage obstacles that can get in the way.

5. **Equality**
    - Treat everyone as an equal.

6. **Express Feelings**
    - Build relationships by sharing honest feelings and thoughts as long as it doe not offend others.

7. **Support**
    - Support helps to build relationships.
    - Support shows you care about others.
    - Support builds strength and reassurance.

8. **Informal Interactions**
    - Identify something you may have in common such as career goals, hobby, vacation places, a pet or sport.

- Hold meetings in a neutral comfortable setting.
- When people feel relaxed they speak more freely.

9. Differences
- Face differences openly and directly.
- Stretch discomfort in an attempt to understand and respect differences.

10. Healthy Conflict Resolution
- Resolve conflict with respect for each others perspective.

11. Goals
- Work towards goals where both parties win.
- A win-win solution builds strong meaningful relationships.

STRATEGY 6

Real Work Life Stress Management
Six Stress Management Strategies

There are effective strategies to assist you in controlling stress at work and in your personal life. Being able to manage your frustrations and behavior will help you manage your emotions in a way that is positive and non-disruptive for others. Understand the triggers that create unhealthy responses and how to reduce stress when things are out of your control.

SIX STRESS MANAGEMENT STRATEGIES

Strategy 1: Acceptance

Accept your present situation and use strategies to help you manage stress.

Strategy 2: Remove Yourself

Remove yourself from the situation that causes stress and take a time-out is a simple and effective stress management strategy. Take a walk or do some form of activity that will help you to relax without disturbing others.

Strategy 3: Relax

Relax by choosing to write, read, sitting silently or listening to music will help you to tune-out the situation and calm down.

Strategy 4: Recognize

Recognize uncontrollable stress and identify the source it comes from. Work towards controlling behavior is the first step in managing confusion, emotions, envy, fear, frustration, sadness and others.

Strategy 5: Reflecting

Reflecting on situations that caused you to react in a negative way will help you to identify a solution to manage this behavior and avoid it in the future.

Strategy 6: Confront

Before confronting a person – identify the root of the problem and the reason for the stress. Work towards calmly addressing the situation by using strategies that will help you go from stress to acceptance.

Unhealthy Anger Indicators

- Activities – Spending too much personal time on the computer, watching too much television, substance abuse and others.
- Critical of Others – Very critical of others.
- Silent Treatment – Giving the silent treatment at work and personal situations.
- Working Excessive Overtime – Spending a lot of time working and not allowing time for you.
- Replaying the Event – Replaying the event that triggered the situation mentally over and over again.
- Revenge Fantasies – Fantasying over and over how you can get revenge.
- Using Profanity – Using profanity at work and personal situations.
- Lashing Out at Others – Losing your temper and lashing out at others.
- Passive – Aggressive Behavior – Expressing stressful behavior at the same time saying you are not stressed.

STRATEGY 7

Communication Strategies for Technical Professionals

Eleven Ways to Improve Relationships with Non-Technical Professionals

Technical professionals could benefit by spending time working with non-technical users to learn how to effectively communicate in language they understand. Good communication, building relationships, writing and presentation skills will help close the communication gap. A combination of technical skills, communication skills and sincere interest will improve business and customer relationships.

Eleven Ways to Improve Relationships with Non-Technical Professionals

1. Communicate Effectively – Clear and effective communication with non-technical people will improve relationships.

2. Actively Listen – Actively listen and be patient with the user.

3. Ask Questions – Ask questions to gather as much information as possible.

4. Confirm– Confirm what you believe is the problem in simple terms to the user.

5. Business Writing– Learn to write technical proposals and reports that can be understood by non-technical users. Use visual aids such as charts and diagrams to illustrate key points.

6. Productivity – Improved communication will increase productivity.
7. Lead Others – Lead others in small initiatives will strengthen your relationships and improve your position.
8. Volunteer to Do More – Volunteer for leadership roles to increase your visibility.
9. Committees – Volunteer to be on committees and expand your non-technical network.
10. Keep Learning – Take a leadership or teambuilding class that will increase your knowledge and provide insight about issues that affect your co-workers.
11. Understand the Business – Subscribe to business magazines so you can speak to customers and co-workers about industry trends.

STRATEGY 8
Ten Rules for Active Listening

Active listening is twice as hard as talking because it takes practice to acquire good listening skills. Information is sent by a speaker and received by an active listener. By moving your face and keeping your eyes on the speaker you can easily adapt good listening skills. An open mind will let you concentrate on the message and receive information. Listed are rules to strengthen your listening skills.

Rule 1: Look

- Look at the person who is speaking.

Rule 2: Eye Contact

- Establish eye contact with the speaker.

Rule 3: Body Language

- Good listeners lead with their facial expressions and body language.

Rule 4: Concentrate

- Concentrate on the message.

Rule 5: Distractions

- Eliminate external distractions.

Rule 6: Write

- Write down questions you may need to ask.

Rule 7: Evaluate

- Evaluate the message delivered.

Rule 8: Conclusions

- Do not jump to conclusions.

Rule 9: Listen

- Do not stop listening.

Rule 10: Verbal and Nonverbal Cues

- Be alert to verbal and nonverbal cues by the speaker.

STRATEGY 9
The Power of Positive Body Language

Body language is a nonverbal form of communication by which your expressions, gestures, and movements convey unspoken messages to those around you. Workplace body language can change how others perceive you and is critical to your career success. Your nonverbal body language may differ depending on what culture you are addressing. When working with people of different cultures it might be useful for you to understand nonverbal body language from multiple cultures.

Although you might think others do not notice you and the messages you are sending your body language does not go unnoticed. Listed are tips for positive and less effective body language and how to best use or avoid them.

Nine Secrets for Success

1. Eye Contact – Make positive direct eye contact with others.

2. Head – Hold your head up straight.
3. Posture – Stand-or-sit tall with your shoulders back. Exude charisma, competence, confidence and power.
4. Hands – Use purposeful hand gestures.
5. Attitude – Your attitude starts on the inside and shows on the outside.
6. Personal Space – Allow 15-20 inches of personal space between you and others.
7. Walk – Walk with confidence, ease and grace.
8. Body Movement – Move your body confidently and gracefully.
9. Smile – Have an engaging smile and light up the room.

Eight Body Language Tips to Avoid

1. Eyes – Rolling your eyes at others.
2. Clenching Fists – Communicates you are experiencing tension or anxiety.
3. Arms – Arms crossed over your chest can be viewed as defensive.
4. Neck Movements – Shows lack of controlled behavior and inappropriate in the workplace.
5. Finger Snapping and Arm Movements – Unprofessional and inappropriate.
6. Hands on Hips – This can translate – "I'm not in agreement with what you are saying."
7. Touching Others – Touching others although the intention may be friendly could be misinterpreted.

If you touch another person observe their reaction to see how your contact affects them. You might consider asking them how they feel when you touch them or perhaps just not touch at all.

8. Barriers – Standing behind a chair or podium, crossing your arms over your chest or speaking to someone behind a computer creates a barrier to communication.

STRATEGY 10

Workplace Negotiation
Ten Steps to Get What You Want

For many professionals negotiation is their most difficult task at work. The ability to negotiate can make the difference between your success or failure for your organization. The key to being successful at negotiations is for both parties to discuss what they want up front – then proceed in the negotiation process. Negotiation requires essential steps for both parties to achieve a win-win solution and achieve their desired goals. Listed are steps that will ensure a successful outcome.

TEN STEPS TO GET WHAT YOU WANT

Step 1: Listen
- Negotiators are good listeners.
- You will find out everything you need to know if you listen.

Step 2: Do Your Home Work

- Gather as much information prior to the negotiation process.
- What are their goals?
- What options do they have?

Step 3: Ask for What You Want

- Be assertive and ask for what you want.
- Express your feelings without anger or anxiety.
- Do not take everything for face value – be prepared to ask questions and challenge those things that you do not believe.
- Everything is negotiable.

Step 4: Expect More

- If you expect more – you will get more.
- Low expectations will result in an undesired outcome.

Step 5: Be Willing to Walk Away

- Never negotiate without options.
- Never lose your ability to say NO.
- Do not accept the other side's demands simply to make a deal.
- If you do not show you are desperate the other side will sense your strength.

Step 6: Take your Time
- Be patient.
- Do not rush the process.
- The negotiator that is more flexible about time will have the advantage.
- The negotiator that has time will likely offer the opposite side concessions as a means for them to say YES.

Step 7: Pressure
- Focus on your negotiators pressure – do not concentrate on your limitations.
- Recognize the reasons for the other negotiator to give-in.
- Be a detective – identify their concerns and worries.
- Take a time out if necessary to regroup.

Step 8: Seek to Understand the Other's Needs
- Seek to understand the other negotiator.
- Be open and see the negotiation from the other side's perspective.
- Help the other negotiator feel satisfied – in exchange they will be more inclined to help you achieve your goals.

Step 9: Behavior
- Do not take the other negotiators behavior personally.

- Try to understand behaviors that are rude or difficult.
- Do not obsess over things that are not directly related to the negotiation issues.

Step 10: Win-Win Solution
- Let the other side earn what you are giving.
- Do not give anything away without getting something in return.
- Achieve the goal of negotiation a win-win solution.

STRATEGY 11

Better Business Writing
Ten Tips for Successful Communication

Today's business world is information driven. Whether you work for an organization or have your own business, the majority of your communication with others will be in writing.

Good writing skills will increase your chances of gaining employment and promotional opportunities at work. Most on-line employers require a cover letter with your application. The purpose of this strategy is to focus only on applicants who can communicate their skills in writing. In the workplace good communication is vital to good business relationships and reduces misunderstandings.

The ability to effectively communicate your thoughts in writing will enhance your career success. Listed are tips to learn to write well.

TEN TIPS FOR SUCCESSFUL COMMUNICATION

1. Keep it Simple

- Make your point immediately – say what you have to say.
- Use words sparingly.
- Avoid long sentences.
- Ask if you do not understand.

2. Avoid Jargon

- Use language that all cultures can understand.

3. Write Once, Check Three Times

- Proofread after you write – do not rely on spell-check.
- Allow time to proofread by setting your document aside to review.
- Our brain is tricky – we tend to read what we want to be there instead of what is written.
- Walk away for a few minutes and then re-read it out loud.

4. Check Your Tone

- When you read your message out loud - it helps you hear your tone.
- Make sure you say what you want it to say and how you want it communicated.

5. Names, Genders and Titles

- If you are not positive of a spelling of persons name, gender or title confirm with someone who know them before you write your document.
- Address people by their formal name until you know if they prefer a nickname.
- A signature on a document gives you permission to address a person by the name signed.
- Do not take it upon yourself to call someone by a nickname you have chosen for them.

6. Be Professional

- Informal communication does not mean unprofessional.
- Do not use jokes – it might be misinterpreted.
- Do not talk about others.
- Be aware – your email may be forwarded to others.
- Most businesses keep copies of all written communication.

7. Remember - Who? What? When? Where? Why? and How?

- Who is the audience that will receive the memo?
- What should they know?
- When and Where it will apply?
- Why it is important?
- How should they use the information you provided?

8. Call to Action

- What is the reader expected to do?
- When should they do it?
- When do you expect a response?

9. Limit Options

- To schedule an appointment or meeting give a maximum of two options.
- Ask for a confirmation of which option.

10. Describe the Benefits

- Why should the reader care?
- Provide benefits that will engage the reader.

STRATEGY 12

Powerful Leadership Communication Skills
Twenty One Laws of Leadership

A leader who can master leadership communication skills will be able to lead their organizations through today's challenges and accomplish its goals. An effective leader can use the following laws as a guideline to communicate.

Twenty One Laws of Leadership
1. *Positive* attitude.
2. *Think we, not I.* Accomplish goals for group success not for personal gain.
3. *Connect* with the person or audience.
4. Establishes *trust* and *respect* of those they lead.
5. Builds *morale* and manages conflict.
6. *Listen* to understand the person or audience.
7. *Generous* in your time and concern for employees and customers.
8. *Inspire* employees to work hard.
9. *Encourage* people to *work together* and accept differences.
10. Master of *emotional control* in your body language.
11. *Confident* communication style.
12. *Engages* people so they are relaxed.
13. *Public speaking* and *presentation skills*.

14. Maintain *authority* and *charisma* when communicating.
15. *Actions* speak louder than words.
16. *Effectively communicates* to all levels of the organization.
17. *Invest* in good communication to minimize grapevine news.
18. 80/20 Rule – 80% of the time *communication* influences people and 20% of *information* informs people.
19. *Listene*r feels you understand them.
20. Have a *distinctive* communication style.
21. Leader's communication consists of three elements:

    1. Physical Appearance and Body Language – 55%
    2. Vocal Tone, Pace and Voice – 38%
    3. Verbal Communication – 7%

Leaders who communicate for maximum impact should use appearance and body language to their advantage. They should manage their tone, voice and verbal communication skills.

STRATEGY 13

Public Speaking
Why Public Speaking is Essential to Your Career Success

Public Speaking is a requirement to get hired, promote yourself, present ideas, products and services and to make you stand out. When you compete for employment or seek a promotion you need dynamic and effective skills to present what you have to offer. To sell yourself at work or in business you need to be able to confidently communicate ideas and thoughts to management, peers, business associates, clients and customers.

Today there are really are no situations where you are not using public speaking skills to communicate. Public Speaking is no longer a value-added skill; it's a core competency skill which is expected in the workplace. The benefits of public speaking skills include career advancement and improved business relationships.

Ask your human resources department about speaking organizations that might meet at your facility. Some speaking organizations have local chapters you can join in your community to enhance your skills. Listed are simple steps to help you speak for success.

Seven Simple Steps to Speak Easy

1. *Join* a professional speaking organization.
2. *Organize* your presentation before you present to an audience.
3. Always *practice out loud* several times before you present anything important to a group or

individual. Practice improves your speaking and presentation skills.

4. *Volunteer* to present to small groups 1-5 people to build confidence and comfort.
5. *Do your homework*. You are the expert on the topic you are presenting. Be prepared to answer questions and over come objections to your ideas.
6. Ask for *feedback* from management and someone you trust such as a mentor.
7. *Public speaking* improves your skills and positions you for the future.

SUMMARY

Effective interpersonal communication skills are important to accomplish the goals and objectives of the organization. Being able to communicate is essential if you want to build a successful career.

Written communication should be clearly written. Verbal communication should be clearly stated. Good interpersonal skills allow you to build relationships, understand people better, manage difficult encounters, overcome barriers, work well in a team environment and develop skills you need to get promoted.

Whether you are pitching and idea to your manager, co-worker or a customer you should have effective selling and presentation skills. Being confident and comfortable communicating your ideas, products or services to internal and external customers will contribute to your success.

When you master the art of good interpersonal communication you will see the rewards at work and in your personal life.

CHAPTER TWELVE
The Power of Personal Accountability

Are you accountable and responsible for your work?

Personal accountability is an important business skill. Employees are expected to take ownership of assigned tasks and results without making excuses for outcomes that are not positive. Your accountability and responsibility impacts the performance, productivity and profitability of the organization. Listed are ways personal accountability affects your performance in the workplace.

20 Personal Accountability Principles

1. Accountability keeps you grounded and reminds you of your responsibility.
2. Mistakes – Admit your mistakes and be willing to do whatever it takes to correct the situation.
3. Correction – Accept correction and do not be rebellious.
4. Avoid Gossip – Spreading gossip about others can hurt their reputation and damage relationships.

5. Choose Your Battles – Use wisdom in making a decision which issues are worth the effort and those that are not. Not every issue is important enough to be fought.
6. Commitments are meant to be kept.
7. Conflict is inevitable the way you respond is your choice.
8. Go The Extra Mile – When asked by management to work overtime go the extra mile to get the job done.
9. Integrity – Make the right choice when faced with a dishonest act.
10. Listen and be open to advice from management and co-workers.
11. Manage Your Words – Speak wisely and positively about co-workers and management.
12. Recognize Your Personal Power – Use personal power to manage your career and achieve the skills required to be successful. No one can give you personal power or take it away but you.
13. Reputation – A good reputation is more valuable than money and power.
14. Respect – Set your standard by respecting others whether they respect you or not.
15. Self-Control – Reserve your thoughts and emotions in certain situations. Take time to process information before you react to make a wise decision.
16. Self Development – Enhance your skill set by taking professional development courses.

17. Take Ownership – Personal accountability and responsibility prevents the "blame game" when tasks and projects are assigned to you.
18. Teamwork – Work with your team and learn from differences, shared goals, benefits and celebrate the rewards.
19. Toot Your Horn – In a professional manner and at the right time let management know of your talents, achievements and how they contributed to the success of your department.
20. Visibility – Be visible at meetings, sit up front to the right of the speaker, speak up and make a contribution, and volunteer to pass out handouts. Take the initiative to take on new challenges, volunteer for a new project or help a co-worker complete a project. Arrive early to work and stay late when possible.

Every employee is accountable and responsible for performing their jobs at the highest standards for their organizations. Personal accountability takes courage, integrity, self confidence and self-examination. Accountability promotes your professionalism, distinguishes you from others and is essential to your success.

CHAPTER THIRTEEN
Intercultural Diversity Skills

Diversity enhances knowledge and learning in the workplace. Employees are encouraged to broaden their perspectives regarding cultural similarities which promote professionalism.

The ability to maximize the knowledge, skills and abilities of multicultural workgroups contributes to professional growth and organizational goals. Listed are diversity skills to help you excel in your position.

Diversity Skills Allow You To:

- Acknowledge and focus on similarities not differences.
- Broaden your cultural perspectives.
- Use cultural-specific knowledge to resolve conflict.
- Enhance knowledge and learning.
- Respect and value other people contributions.
- Communicate effectively with individuals and diverse groups.

- Increase innovation and productivity for the organization.
- Listen and interpret with an open mind.
- Make decisions that will unite all employees.
- Promote understanding of others' perceptions in a multicultural environment.

Intercultural diversity skills promote appreciation for talents and skills which are essential for career success.

CHAPTER FOURTEEN
Time Management Strategies
Assessing Your Relationship with Time

Establishing your relationship with time is an important part of learning to use time wisely. Everyone's relationship with time is different; therefore, all strategies for managing time will vary accordingly.

Your strengths, weaknesses, commitments, lifestyle, and responsibilities all play a role in your time management strategy.

Priorities

- Identify your work priorities.
- Write down your priorities; be specific as possible.
- Rank the importance of multiple priorities.
- Too many priorities at the same time will increase stress.

Goals

- Translate your priorities into goals.
- Break each goal into activities and identify the steps needed to achieve the goal.
- Identify resources needed to accomplish your goal; you might require the assistance of other people.

Planning

- Use a monthly calendar. Your monthly calendar or notebook is a time-saving device. Consistent use of your calendar provides a visual reminder of your commitments.
- Identify work-related goals, such as weekly, monthly, or quarterly reports, and add them to your calendar.
- Schedule important activities such as teleconferences, webinars, meetings, appointments, due dates, and deadlines and add them to your calendar. Scheduling deadlines gives you direction and confirms your commitment to meet deadlines.
- Plan time in your calendar to review and accomplish deadlines, but do not wait until the day before a deadline occurs.
- Highlight important dates and reports on your calendar in color.

Personal Time Management Barriers
- Do you feel "too controlled?"
- Is the task you need to accomplish boring?
- Identify your own barriers to effective time management.

Achieve "Meaningful" Outcomes
- Effective time management will assist you in achieving meaningful outcomes, not more outcomes.

CHAPTER FIFTEEN
Successful Strategies for Dealing with Difficult Behaviors

INTRODUCTION

Communication skills are the foundation and most important soft skill you can learn. Successful strategies for dealing with difficult behavior suggest *logical* action instead of *emotionally* reacting to difficult situations. Your career and personal success will be determined how effectively you communicate with your co-workers, managers and others. To work effectively with all types of people and personalities you need specific communication skills to help you when things are not going well. Once you learn coping strategies, communication techniques, how to manage anxiety, emotional self-control, and how to rebuild relationships and others you will be better equipped to manage difficult encounters. Losing control of your temper blocks good judgment and does not resolve the issues.

Communication strategies provide specific techniques for dealing with difficult behaviors with tact and skill. Knowing which approach to use will allow you to enjoy your job, co-workers, managers, and personal relationships with professionalism and confidence.

Difficult People

Difficult people may take their anger out on you; hide their inferior feelings and anxiety by acting aggressive and superior to others. Focus on how to deal with difficult behavior and get the desired results to be professional, successful and accomplish your goals.

STRATEGY 1

Coping with Difficult Behavior

Six Steps for Coping with Difficult Behavior

Step 1: Assess

- Assess whether the *situation or person* is the reason for the behavior.

Step 2: Stop

- Stop wishing the person's behavior would be acceptable.

Step 3: Distance

- Distance yourself from the behavior when you can.

Step 4: Coping Plan
- A coping plan is a necessary tool to have available at all times.

Step 5: Implement
- Implement your plan.

Step 6: Monitor
- Monitor the results for effectiveness.

STRATEGY 2

How to Resolve Conflict

Anyone can learn skills required to resolve conflict. The skills involved in resolving and managing conflict can have a positive effect on professional and personal relationships.

Four Easy Steps to Resolve Conflict

Step 1: Active Listening
- Active listening is restating in your own words, what you believe the other person has said.
- Active listening is a way for you to confirm your understanding of what has been said.

Step 2: Situation

- Evaluate the current *situation.*

Step 3: Target

- Identify the *target* – the preferred behavior situation.

Step 4: Action Plan

- *Plan* a strategy to get you from the existing difficult behavior to the *target situation.*

STRATEGY 3

Conflict De-Escalation Strategies

Everyone has experience being in an argument that has escalated out of control. Listed are action strategies to help you de-escalate a conflict with others.

Eight Conflict De-Escalation Strategies

Strategy 1: Acknowledge

- Show respect by acknowledging the other persons point of view.

Strategy 2: Be Specific
- Speak specifically to your point, present the facts and avoid generalities.

Strategy 3: Body Language
- Avoid using hostile and inappropriate body language such as, rolling eyes, crossing arms in front of your body, tapping your foot, neck movements, snapping of fingers and waving arms.

Strategy 4: "I" and "You"
- Use "I" and avoid using "You" statements when speaking.

Strategy 5: Name Calling
- Avoid name-calling and put-downs.

Strategy 6: Physical
- Avoid getting physical with anyone. Do not get in their personal space – stand at an appropriate distance.

Strategy 7: Time Out
- Take an agreed upon time out to calm down.

Strategy 8: Tone
- Soften your tone – do not raise your voice.

STRATEGY 4

Effective Ways to Manage Conflict

When people get together at work or personal situations, conflict can be a reality because of our differences in our interests and personality. When conflict is managed the result can benefit all parties.

Anger is a Human and Natural Emotion

- Expressing anger can be positive if it can be done constructively without hurting yourself and others.
- Accept responsibility for your emotions and actions.
- Find non-violent ways to express your anger (i.e., walking, riding a bike, exercising).
- Tell others how you feel without becoming abusive.
- Verbal attacks can increase difficult behavior.
- Stay *calm* and in *control.*

STRATEGY 5

How to Increase Positive Behavior in Others

Three Communication Techniques
1. Positive Communication
- Identify and praise positive behavior.

Positive Communication Message

Verbal...
Non-Verbal...

Saying "Thank You"
Smiling

Telling someone else
A Nod of Approval

Saying "Good", "Fantastic" or "Great"
Clapping

A Message of "Appreciation"
Shaking Hands

2. Track Communication
- Look for praise and track positive behavior.

3. Reinforce Communication
- Be sincere and reinforce approved behavior.

STRATEGY 6

Three Strategies for Difficult Encounters

Strategy 1: Aggressive

- Look out for *#1* before anyone else.

Strategy 2: Non-Assertive

- Always consider *others before* yourself.

Strategy 3: Assertive

- Look out for #1 but be *kind* and *considerate* of others.

STRATEGY 7

Manage Anxiety in Difficult Situations

Four Tips to Manage Anxiety

Tip 1: Identify

- Identify the situations that increase your heart rate, breathing and other physical changes.

Tip 2: List

- List the situation or other valuable information that creates uncomfortable feelings.

Tip 3: Plan

- Devise a plan to acknowledge and overcome your anxieties.

Tip 4: Prioritize

- Prioritize your anxieties that affect how you feel.

STRATEGY 8

Emotional Self-Control

Six Effective Emotional Self-Control Techniques

Technique 1 – Walk Away

- Walk away from the situation and do not try to have the last word.

Technique 2 – Count

- Count to 20 when 10 is not long enough. Take time to think and process what is being said before you speak.

Technique 3 – Consult

- Consult a neutral party and ask for feedback. Be open to critique if it means you were wrong and could have handled the situation in a professional manner. The goal is to learn from the experience.

Technique 4 – Acknowledge

- Acknowledge and calmly express your emotions.

Technique 5 – Accept Responsibility
- Accept responsibility and apologize if you are responsible for the situation.

Technique 6 – Prepare
- Prepare yourself for a potentially emotional situation.

STRATEGY 9

How to Maintain Relationships with Chronically Difficult Behaviors

- Avoid the *spiral effect* of reciprocating difficult behavior.
- Commit to a *positive* working relationship with the other person.
- Keep *honest* and *open* communication.
- Treat others with *unconditional respect*.
- Do not *overestimate* your understanding of other's behavior.
- Listen and watch for *nonverbal* behavior cues.
- Accept and deal with difficult people *confidently* and *seriously*.

- *Ask questions* to determine the motivation of the other person's behavior.

STRATEGY 10

Rebuilding a Damaged Relationship

The most important strategy to pursue in a conflict is a win-win situation. The belief is although there may be differences a solution is possible.

Seven Steps for Rebuilding a Damaged Relationship

Step 1: *Calmly* confront the problem.

Step 2: Avoid *"I win"* and *"You lose"* situations – seek a "Win-Win" solution.

Step 3: Be *consistent* in your information.

Step 4: Be *honest, sincere*, and *direct* when you communicate.

Step 5: Accept *responsibility* for your behavior and feelings.

Step 6: Adopt an *exchange system* that will help you express your feelings.

Step 7: Commit to the same *goal* of improving the relationship.

STRATEGY 11

When your Manager is a Difficult Person

To deal with a difficult manager confidently and effectively you need a systematic approach to produce positive change in their behavior. Use these strategies to manage different types of managers and their behavior.

Bully Behavior

Managers who are bullies tend to be inflexible and overbearing.

Coping Strategies

- Present your case calmly and confidently.
- Be prepared to answer the "why" for decisions you make with supportive data.
- Build trust and confidence in your abilities.

Micro-Manager

The micro-manager wants to know in detail how you spend your time. Some managers may resist giving you challenging assignments for fear of losing control.

Coping Strategies

- Ask yourself if you have done anything to undermine their confidence in you.
- Work to build their trust.
- Keep your manager informed on a regular basis.

- In time, your manager will gain confidence in your abilities and will be less controlling.

STRATEGY 12

Seven Strategies to Manage a Difficult Manager

Strategy 1: Control your Emotions

- Do not react to criticism and verbal abuse with emotion.
- Remain calm.
- Listen to what is being said.
- By listening and not reacting you maintain your control and emotions.

Strategy 2: Discuss Rather than Confront Criticism

- Do not become confrontational this breeds more conflict.
- Use constructive criticism to discuss goals, interests and problem-solve. Ask for advice for improvement.

Strategy 3: Manage your New Manager

- Be proactive and ask up front how a new manager wants things done.
- Being proactive avoids miscommunication.
- Find out what their likes and dislikes are so you can avoid conflict.

Strategy 4: Be Professional

- Keep your professional attitude and face on at all times.
- You do not have to like your manager – but you should always be professional.
- Focus on getting the job done and implementing their instructions.

Strategy 5: Self-Evaluation

- Consider evaluating your own performance.
- Ask yourself if you are doing what you are suppose to do and if you are doing it right.
- Ask yourself and your supervisor if there is room for improvement.

Strategy 6: Chain of Command

- Do not go to the top of the chain of command unless it's a last resort.
- Going straight to the top could be a career limiting move and increases conflict.
- Discuss concerns with your manager first and only go up the chain of command if you have exhausted all other options.

Strategy 7: Leave Work at Work

- Make it a habit to leave work at work and not bring it home.
- Separate your personal life from your work life.

- Have friends who do not work with you so the tendency is not to discuss work.

SUMMARY

Almost everyone has encountered difficult people at work, in personal situations and the frustrations of interacting and communicating with them. By learning and applying various difficult behavior strategies, techniques and tips you make it impossible for these behaviors to control your attitude. Use strategies to create positive change in your relationships and deal with people more effectively.

The communication choices you use will determine whether your action is logical rather than emotional. The most effective way to manage conflict is to take a proactive approach to manage the process for positive outcomes.

CHAPTER SIXTEEN
Teamwork Strategies

Teamwork is bringing people together for the common purpose of maintaining and improving team member interactions within an organization. Listed are teamwork strategies, empowerment tips and people skills to contribute to your organizational goals.

Ten Teamwork Strategies

1. Know each employee and their abilities.
2. Give clear directions and confirm they understand.
3. Allow employees to make decisions related to their work.
4. Be accessible and listen to their input.
5. Praise and reward employees accordingly.
6. Treat all employees fairly and with respect.
7. Show sincere interest and concern for all employees.
8. Make each employee an integral member of the team.

9. Keep employees challenged and excited about their work.

10. Support employees in their efforts to achieve maximum performance.

TEN WAYS TO EMPOWER YOUR TEAM

Empowering your team is a practical way to get things accomplished. When a team is empowered it builds trust, performance and the ability for the organization to learn from successes and mistakes.

1. Assign tasks. Assign tasks to employees to encourage them to grow and accept additional responsibilities.

2. Information. Provide information about the task and let employees know what's in it for them – what the purpose is for the completed task.

3. Communication. Provide clear directions, details and confirm everyone understands.

4. Ask Questions. Encourage employees to ask questions to determine what to do and extend thinking.

5. Explain Why. When you explain why a task is done it will reduce the number of questions.

6. Authority and Resources. Give employees the authority and resources to get things done.

7. Creativity. Solicit suggestions for efficient ways of getting things done.

8. Time Management. Target a realistic due date and monitor progress.
9. Establish Priorities. Explain what needs to be done first and why so you will gain commitment.
10. Follow-up. Be accessible when your team needs assistance. Be careful not to micro-manage.

Teamwork People Skills

Personality. Learn employee's personalities and what motivates them and their behavior.

Exceptional Traits. Identify exceptional straits that separate one employee from another.

Opportunity. Assign tasks that will increase professional development opportunities.

Participation. Ask employees to participate in the decision making of their assignments.

Leadership. Lead and motivate employees to achieve organizational goals.

Expectations. Inform employees about expectations and performance standards.

CHAPTER SEVENTEEN
Problem Solving Strategies

Are you a problem solver?

Problem-solving skills are an important tool every professional needs to achieve organizational goals. Use the PAR Formula action steps to – identify the problem, take action and achieve results. Listed are questions to consider within each step to use as a guide to problem solve.

**THE PAR FORMULA
(PROBLEM, ACTION AND RESULTS)**

Three Steps to Problem Solving

Step 1: Problem – Define the Problem Clearly
1. What is the problem?
2. Did you identify the problem or was it brought to your attention?
3. Why did this problem occur?

4. Is this a reoccurring problem?
5. Who does this problem affect?

Step 2: Action – Develop an Action Plan

1. What action steps will you use to solve the problem?
2. What are your options?
3. What do you need to solve the problem?
4. Can you solve the problem alone or will you need assistance?
5. Are there costs associated with solving the problem?
6. Is there time or other barriers associated with solving the problem?
7. Can you solve the problem without management approval? Are you a risk taker?
8. If your plan requires management approval – how will you present and support your action plan?
9. Can I implement my plan immediately or will I need to set a target date?
10. Who will I need to inform the problem is solved?

Step 3: Results

1. What are the results of your action plan?
2. How well did you solve the problem?
3. What would you do differently? Why?

4. What did you learn that is beneficial to solve future problems?

Problem solving skills will enable you to increase your responsibility, visibility and value to your employer.

CHAPTER EIGHTEEN
Build Good Relationships
Connecting for Career Success

Build Good Relationships with Management

Building relationships with management should be a part of your career development strategy. Managers look for employees who show a sincere interest in setting and achieving goals, self growth, and improvement. Employees who accept additional assignments, volunteer for special projects, and help others position themselves for advancement and management support for new career opportunities.

Seven Management Relationship Strategies

1. Build good relationships with management.
2. Invite your manager or supervisor to breakfast, lunch, break or dinner so they can get to know you.
3. Resolve conflicts.
4. Ask for additional responsibilities.
5. Volunteer for assignments.

6. Be seen as an asset.
7. Develop your management network.

NETWORK AT WORK

Win Inside

No matter where you work building relationships and networking are more important to your career than ever before. Traditional career paths have changed. People must rely on their own ability to build networks to manage their careers.

A network of contacts inside and outside of an organization – in multiple industries is one of the most important things a professional can do to advance their career. To get a promotion, spend more time building relationships.

It's Not Who You Know…It's Who Knows You!

Why Build Relationships at Work?

- Change – Use your network to stay informed about organizational change.
- Profitable Results – Your job depends on the success of the organization.
- Venture – Step into non-traditional career opportunities.
- Collaboration – Increase teamwork with other people and departments.

- Expand Your Knowledge – Create a network of people with different interests and expertise.

Benefits
- Increase visibility. New opportunities will find you.
- Accountability and responsibility. Manage your "own" career.
- Options. Always keep your career and business options open.

Transitional Skills
- Determine a strategy to showcase your skills, abilities, and interest to others.

Networking Thoughts
- What resources do you have to help others?
- What can you offer others in your networking relationship?

Networking As A Way of Life

Networking will bring you personal and professional success. Make the most of your time; be determined, patient, and visible.

Practice conversations with people in familiar and uncommon places. Asking questions is a sign of a good listener and will help you establish rapport and build relationships. Networking has a beginning and no end.

DEVELOP YOUR NETWORK
THE SMARTEST BUSINESS DECISION

"Networking is building relationships, helping others, and giving advice to anyone who asks."
– Patricia Dorch

Listed are networking tips to help you become more successful at networking.

Names – Remember people's names.

Eye – Eye contact is important.

Talk – Talk, but also listen to what is said.

Write – Write follow-up notes on a regular basis.

Open – Be open and ask questions.

Resource – Become a resource for others.

Knowledge – Knowledge is the power to control your destiny.

CHAPTER NINETEEN
Exceptional Customer Service for the Workplace

Customer service can make or break any organization in today's competitive market. Effective communication is the key to exceptional internal and external customer service. Internal customers are co-workers, management and executives within your organization who improve morale, productivity, growth and promote organizational goals. Successful internal customer service can improve satisfaction to external customers who are outside of your organization. Listed are customer service strategies to demonstrate your professionalism and provide a level of service that is expected in the workplace.

Exceptional Customer Service Strategies
C.U.S.T.O.M.E.R

Communication
- Communication includes talking, writing, email, voice mail and body language.

- Develop a customer friendly attitude.
- Ask questions to identify customer needs.

Under Promise and Over Deliver

- Commitments achieved ahead of schedule make you and your organization look good.
- Only promise customers what you can confidently deliver.
- If you cannot deliver on a promise of service notify the customer and provide an explanation and possible options.

Stress

The demands of your job can increase stress in the workplace. Use these useful tips to provide service, work smart and stress less.

- Manage your time.
- Do not over commit your schedule.
- Prepare a daily to do list.
- Set daily priorities and pace yourself.
- Allow time for unexpected service interruptions or projects.
- Be flexible and adapt to change.

Telephone Calls

- Always have pen and paper available to take notes when you place or take a telephone call.

Chapter Nineteen: Exceptional Customer Service for the Workplace

- Smile and be friendly when you are on the telephone.
- If you do not know the customer, ask for their full name, area code and telephone number.
- Use the caller's name during your conversation makes the call more personal.
- Provide your customer with your full name and contact information.

Options

- When you have to say *no* to a customer's request offer at least two options to show them you are trying to provide customer service.

Memorable

- Memorable customer service builds a professional reputation and keeps customers coming back to you and your organization.

Empathy Phrases

At some point in your career you will encounter an unhappy customer, when this happens express your empathy for the circumstance. Whether you agree with the customer or not, the key is understanding what a customer wants to hear from you is empathy. Consider these empathy phrases to express your support.

- I'm sorry that happened to you.
- I'm sorry you feel that way.
- I'm sorry to hear that.

- I understand your point of view.
- How can I help you in this situation?

Relationships
- Establishing trusting relationships is essential to customer service.

S.E.R.V.I.C.E

Solution
- Solving the customer's problem or concern is important in providing customer service.

External Customers
- Actively listen to the customers needs.
- Be courteous, respectful and positive during every interaction.
- Do not interrupt the customer when they are speaking.
- Ask clarifying questions to better assess how to help them.
- Be knowledgeable about your company's products and services.
- Tell customers what they want to know not everything you know.

- Be able to offer recommendations.
- Close the conversation by asking if there is anything else you can do to help them.

Reliable

- Being reliable shows respect for others and your professionalism.
- Be on time for all commitments.
- If you think you will be late for commitments notify your contacts. Provide an estimated time you will be available.
- Do not wait until the last minute to notify your contacts of your delay.

Vocal Tone

- Your vocal tone is 86% of your conversation with a customer.
- Your vocal tone should be positive and upbeat.
- It's not what you say; it's how you say it.

Internal Customers

- Identify key internal customers.
- Identify the level of service you need to provide to achieve their expectations.
- If you cannot provide a customer with a request extend customer service by finding out whom you can refer them to for help.

Commitment

- Keep commitments.
- Take the necessary action discussed about commitments.

Ending the Telephone Call

- Summarize actions steps discussed in your conversation to ensure customer satisfaction.
- Ask the customer if you can provide any additional service.
- End the telephone call on a positive note.
- Thank your customer for the call if they called you.
- Review important notes you took during the telephone call.
- Implement action steps you discussed.

Customer service begins with you and is not limited to any group of employee's at work assigned to department or call service center. Every interaction with internal and external customers is important to your job and the responsibility of all employees.

CHAPTER TWENTY

How to Resign with Grace and Class

INTRODUCTION

Starting a new career is an exciting time. When you resign from your current employer – no matter what your reason do so with grace and class. When faced with a situation that is not favorable remain professional. Use these resignation guidelines to make your transition a positive experience for your employer.

Fourteen Resignation Rules:

Rule 1 – Employer's Resignation Policy

- Read your employee's handbook regarding the resignation policy.

Rule 2 – When to Give Notice

- Give your resignation notice to your current employer after you have received a "Letter of Offer" from your new employer.

Rule 3 – Letter of Resignation

- Date your resignation letter.
- Personalized your resignation letter – do not use a template.
- State your last day of employment.
- Give a minimum two weeks notice in writing to your employer.
- Do not state your resignation without your written notice in your hand to present to your manager.
- Keep a copy for your personal file.

Rule 4 – Meet with Your Manager

- Give your resignation notice to your manager before you tell co-workers or put it on a social networking site.
- Thank your manager for the career opportunity.

Rule 5 – Assignments and Projects

- Ask your manager to provide you a list of what they would like you to accomplish before you leave.
- Ask about priorities for assignments and projects.
- Tie up loose ends to ensure your transition will be smooth for your manager and make you look good.

Rule 6 – Letter of Reference

- Once you give your resignation notice and depending on your relationship with your manager – ask for a letter of reference.
- Request the letter of reference be written on company letterhead – this makes it more official.

Rule 7 – Competitor Information

- Some employer policies require you leave immediately if you are going to work for a competitor.
- If you disclose your new employer information to your manager – you may ask it be kept confidential.

Rule 8 – Be Prepared

- Take a box for your personal belongings on the day you give your resignation notice.
- If you have a company vehicle clean the car out the day before you give your notice.
- Have a friend or family member on standby to pick you up.

Rule 9 – New Employer Privacy Option

- When asked by co-workers who your new employer is simply say "I prefer not to announce my new employer at this time – I know you will respect my privacy – thank you."
- Keep your discussions general rather than specific details.

- Although you may be excited be careful not to brag about your new career.

Rule 10 – Get Settled in Your New Job

- Allow time for your new employer and co-workers to get acquainted with you without outside influences.

- Protect yourself from possible career sabotage on social networking sites or otherwise before you start a new position. You never know who may not be supportive of your new career.

Rule 11 – Stay Focused

- Stay focused on your current job during your transition time.

- Do not call in sick or take time off unless you absolutely have to once you have given notice.

Rule 12 – Professional Relationships

- Maintain good working relationships - it's possible you may cross the path of people you have worked with in the future.

Rule 13 – Thank-You Note

- Write a personal thank-you note to your manager.

- Thank your manager for the opportunity, value of the experience and career growth.

- Write individual or a group thank-you note to co-workers to express how much you enjoyed working with them.
- Give thank-you notes on your last day or mail them within 48 hours.

Rule 14 – Resign with Grace and Class
- Do all the right things during your transition.
- Resign with professionalism – no matter what the circumstances.

SUMMARY

There may be a time in your career when you are presented with a counter offer from your current employer, a new career opportunity or an offer from a previous manager or colleague. Before you accept any offer take up to forty eight hours to make a decision. During this time carefully evaluate the offer and make a list what you will gain or lose. Compare the offer package to your long-term career and financial goals.

Ask questions and base your decision on the facts of the offer – not emotions. Accept the career opportunity that is aligned with your short and long-term goals. Do not make the career move based only on financial reasons. Separate the position from the person who is offering you the job. Make your move with professionalism, grace and class for the right reasons.

"Career success begins with professionalism."
-PATRICIA DORCH

PROFESSIONALISM
The Smartest Career Decision

Professional Appearance – Influence the opinions and perceptions others have of you.

Respect authority, others and our differences.

Oral and written communication skills are essential to career success.

Follow the corporate chain of command – Never go above your manager and complain.

Ethic – Have a good work ethic and take pride in working hard to achieve goals.

Self Awareness – Understand your personal style and adapt to others.

Sensitive – Be sensitive to others perceptions in a multicultural environment.

Integrity – Make the correct choice when faced with a right or wrong decision.

Only use email, texting, voicemail and the internet for company business.

No Gossiping – Do not indulge in office gossip.

Accountability – Take ownership for results whether they are successful or not.

Learn from constructive criticism and feedback.

Interpersonal Communication skills are important to accomplish professional goals.

Success is a result of hard work and persistence.

Manage your time to meet deadlines and accomplish goals.

Copyright © 2012 Patricia Dorch. All Rights Reserved

> *"Personal and career development is an individual responsibility."*
> -PATRICIA DORCH

PROFESSIONALISM
New Rules for Workplace Career Success

SUMMARY

Professionalism: New Rules for Workplace Career Success is the ultimate career guide for every professional – it offers "how to" knowledge you need in the workplace. This indispensable resource provides skills to enable you to manage your professionalism in many areas to increase your visibility and accelerate your career.

Are you ready for the 21st Century? Life-long learning is crucial for employment to succeed in the new economy. Employees have a responsibility to read books, take classes, attend seminars and webinars, obtain a degree or certificate. Professional growth challenges employees to go outside of your comfort zone – beyond the familiar and close the knowledge and skill gap to compete in the changing workplace.

Today's competitive workforce requires employees take the initiative to learn multiple skill-sets and not solely rely on employers for career training and development.

The regular practice of continuous learning enables employees to be employable, marketable and the key to career advancement and success.

You are invited to write a book review at:

www.amazon.com and www.barnesandnoble.com

Thank your for sharing your feedback.

ABOUT THE AUTHOR

PATRICIA DORCH is President and CEO of EXECU DRESS. She has a Master of Science in Business Organizational Management from the University of LaVerne in LaVerne, California. Patricia has a background in Sales and Marketing for major business, medical and healthcare corporations.

Patricia is the author of *Job Search: New Get Hired Ideas, Tips and Strategies for 40 Plus* and *Six Figure Career Coaching Advice: The Ultimate Guide To Achieving Success.* Patricia is an in-demand career expert who specializes in maximizing the potential for professionals to get hired, demonstrate professionalism in the workplace and get promoted in today's ultra competitive job market.

Are you looking for a speaker? Patricia is a dynamic speaker and trainer – schedule her for your next conference, meeting, regional or local training and career event at:

Website: www.whatisprofessionalism.com
Email: Patricia@whatisprofessionalism.com

Website: www.jobsearch40plusbook.com
Email: Patricia@jobsearch40plusbook.com

Website: www.execudress.com
Email: Patricia@execudress.com

SIX FIGURE
Career
Coaching
Advice

Patricia Dorch

The Ultimate Guide
To Achieving Success

Job Search

New
Get Hired
Ideas, Tips and Strategies for
40 Plus

PATRICIA DORCH

CPSIA information can be obtained at www.ICGtesting.com
Printed in the USA
BVOW02s0048200815

414076BV00016B/331/P